To Milly and Marc,

Thank you for
visiting Seminole.
Hope you enjoy the book.

Mehn

Moving Heaven and Earth

The Life of Melvin Moran

BY KAREN ANSON

FOREWORD BY GOVERNOR BRAD HENRY

OKLAHOMA TRACKMAKER SERIES

SERIES EDITOR: GINI MOORE CAMPBELL

OKLAHOMA TRACKMAKER SERIES

Copyright 2009 by Oklahoma Heritage Association

Printed in the United States of America.

ISBN 978-1-885596-81-9

Library of Congress Catalog Number 2009939306

Designed by Kris Vculek

Unless otherwise noted, photographs are courtesy of Melvin Moran.

CONTENTS

DEDICATION

This book is dedicated to my beloved wife, Jasmine. She has encouraged and participated with me in every activity which I have undertaken.

Melvin Moran

ACKNOWLEDGMENTS

I'd like to thank Melvin Moran for the opportunity to document the life of one of the most fascinating and hilarious people in Oklahoma's history. He made the task so easy, recording his thoughts as he drove in his perilous, haphazard way all over Oklahoma, then asking his secretary Thelma Arnold to transcribe and e-mail them to me. We only needed a few interviews together because Melvin was so thorough in relating his memories.

I must thank Vance Trimble, Oklahoma's Pulitzer Prize winner, for recommending me for this enjoyable task and for his advice on how to get started. He has proved an inspiration throughout the years that I have known him.

All the people I interviewed were so helpful and so willing to put aside time from their busy lives to talk about Melvin. I am under no illusion that they would have done it for this writer, but every one of them would have done anything for Melvin Moran. As would I. And as would almost every person who has ever met him. Saying no to Melvin Moran would be like a personal affront to your grandmother. It's just not done.

I would like to thank the Oklahoma Heritage Association, its board of directors, and Gini Campbell, director of publications, for their dedication to celebrating and promoting the achievements of Oklahomans through the publications program. Melvin Moran is definitely worthy of his story forever being preserved in the Oklahoma Trackmaker Series.

But especially I would thank Lana Reynolds, who compiled information on Melvin's time as an SSC regent, and Robert Henry, who was perhaps the most eloquent person I have ever interviewed, and who, in spite of his hectic schedule, gave this project a priority which made my work much easier. I could have listened to him talk about Melvin Moran forever.

— *Karen Anson*

FOREWORD

By Oklahoma Governor Brad Henry

Anyone who knows Melvin Moran, or is fortunate enough to meet him, is likely to be struck by his friendliness and generous nature. That alone might not sound like a big deal. Such character traits are certainly admirable, but, thankfully, they are not particularly rare.

In Melvin's case, however, his warmth and humility are nearly dazzling. After all, here is a man whose biography is that of the quintessential American success story. In the worlds of business and civic involvement, Melvin Moran has accomplished things about which most of us can only dream.

And yet Melvin remains what he has always been — hardworking, caring, and compassionate. A nice guy. A real *mensch*.

My wife Kim and I have had the privilege of being friends with Melvin Moran for a number of years. We are hardly alone in that regard. Through his energy and forward-thinking vision, Melvin Moran has been a good friend to his home state of Oklahoma. Of his many philanthropic endeavors, perhaps his greatest is the Jasmine Moran Children's Museum, which Melvin and his lovely wife, Jasmine, founded in Seminole, Oklahoma, in 1993. The 36,000-square foot facility is truly one of the state's most beloved treasures, a place where young people learn while having fun.

Melvin holds a special affection for his hometown of Seminole. He served 14 years on its city council and was the town mayor in the late 1970s. More than 30 years ago, he and Jasmine began an annual Christmas dinner for the community's elderly and poor citizens. Melvin's commitment to humanity spans oceans. A devout Jew with a deep and abiding faith, he also has been a strong supporter of Israel's Ben Gurion University.

Melvin knows the unmatched joys that come from helping others. Judaism teaches that the well-being of mankind hinges on tzadikkim, or "righteous people"— people whose idealism, strength of character, and decency protect the world from self-destruction. The Torah teaches that there is no greater goal than to join the ranks of the tzadikkim.

Make no mistake, Melvin Moran is a righteous person of unwavering compassion, integrity, and decency. Throughout his remarkable journey, he has touched the lives of countless others, often moving heaven and earth in his commitment to making the world a better place.

PREFACE

In early 2007, I attended a reception for my good friend, Karen Anson, who was retiring as managing editor of *The Seminole Producer*. At that reception, I had the privilege of meeting Vance Trimble, a noted author. Vance has written several outstanding books, including biographies of Sam Walton and former baseball commissioner Happy Chandler. Shortly after meeting Vance, he said to me, "Melvin, a book should be written about your life." My response was, "No, I don't think so." And Vance then said, "If for no other reason, you should write it for your family." That last remark won me over and I asked Vance if he would be willing to write the book. Vance told me that, because of his diminished eyesight, he is no longer able to write. As an author, he suggested our mutual good friend, Karen Anson. And I loved that suggestion.

I assumed that my wife, our three children, our six grandchildren, and my brother and my sister would likely be interested in reading this book. I was thinking of a publication number of twelve. If you, who are reading this book, do not have the name of Jasmine, Marilyn, Elisa, David, Allison, Julie, Michelle, Nicole, Annika, Ingrid, Sidney, or Jeannie, then sales of this book have exceeded my expectation.

—Melvin Moran

CHAPTER ONE

Anxiety in Israel

"Do it for Dad."

—Melvin Moran

The first indication he had that something was not right was upon waking.

It was December 2, 1981, an important morning for Melvin Moran. One of the most thrilling moments of his life was scheduled for today. He had looked forward to it for months — the dedication and naming of a wing of the Ben-Gurion University's library in his father's honor.

Melvin and his father before him had come to see the Ben-Gurion University as an icon for Israel itself and the asylum that Israel had offered his family after World War II. Both knew that members of their family might never have survived the Holocaust if they had not been able to get out of Latvia to Siberia and then to Israel. The Morans' support of the university had culminated in this wing being built in Meyer Moran's honor, two years after his death.

As his father's eldest son, Melvin had labored over the speech he would give. His wife and oldest daughter had accompanied him to Jerusalem, as well as his brother and sister and their spouses. They were all together, all waking and getting dressed in their hotel rooms, getting ready for the noon-time ceremony.

For a few minutes after waking, Melvin laid

perfectly still, eyes closed, listening as the heater pumped warm air into his room. He felt sweat on his forehead and wondered if the heat was turned up too high. He heard the alarm clock buzz and felt his wife Jasmine turn it off, then rise and begin to dress. He opened his eyes slowly, feeling weak, heart pounding, and noticing that, despite the fact that the heater had switched off, he felt that sunrays were emanating from his forehead. He was as hot as a furnace, almost glowing from the heat, with waves rising from him like from a sun-baked highway. Yet his hands and feet were clammy, chilly. He knew he had a fever — a high one if he was any judge — but he could not be sick today of all days.

Melvin rose and began dressing carefully, slowly. Jasmine chatted about the day, the trip. They had to be downstairs for breakfast at 6:00 a.m. Their daughter Marilyn, 27, came in to ask her mother's opinion about something; she was almost ready.

"Are you all right?" Jasmine asked him and Melvin jumped slightly.

"Yes, yes, I'm fine, why do you ask?" Melvin replied.

"Well, you're so quiet this morning," she said.

"I guess I'm just excited," he answered.

The family went down to breakfast. Melvin's head buzzed; he felt his entire body vibrate with the simple exertion of walking the few steps to the elevator. The little exercise made him feel sweaty and flushed, like he had run for miles. The elevator ride was bumpy and Melvin held on to the rail, hoping his knees would not buckle beneath him. He bit his lip, hoping no one would notice his discomfort.

Downstairs, a buffet was set up on one side of the dining
room with kosher meats, fish, eggs, fruit, and breads. They
joined the rest of their clan at a large round table in the center
of the room. Melvin's brother and sister-in-law, Sid and Ione,
and his sister and brother-in-law, Jeannie and Jerry Tiras, already
were eating.

"Try these rolls," said Jeannie. "They're delicious."

Melvin took a little fruit and juice and sat down. The heat
pouring from his body made him sweat and he was extremely
thirsty. The effort of coming downstairs almost was more than
he could handle. Every muscle in his body ached. Jasmine,
always the observant wife, saw the fine sheen of perspiration
on Melvin's forehead.

"You're not fine," she said, reaching a hand to his forehead. "You're sick. Oh my goodness, you're burning up!"

"I'm fine, really," Melvin said. A little fever was not going
to keep him away from the dedication of his father's wing of the
Ben-Gurion Library.

The event was enormously important in Israel. The library,
similar to American presidential libraries, had been built as an
extension of Ben-Gurion University near the kibbutz where
David Ben-Gurion, the father of Israel, had lived until his death
eight years before. The library was actually a new research center. The dedication would be attended by the members of the
political and educational leadership of the entire country.

Melvin's father had loved Israel and had supported it any
way he could. His support was not just because of his dedication to Judaism, although that was a large part. Meyer had
left Latvia for America as an 18-year-old boy, leaving behind

everyone and everything he had ever known. He had spent years trying to get his family out of Latvia and he had managed to bring most of them to his new country. The last of them, Meyer's oldest sister, Sonia, and her family, fled Latvia before the Nazis arrived. After spending World War II in Siberia, they sought refuge in Israel. Many members of Melvin's family still live in Israel today. Meyer's gratitude for the country's humanitarianism to his family was enormous.

Melvin had no intention of letting his father down. He had loved the man and spent his life trying to make him and his mother proud. Today he would stand up before the most important figures in Israel's history and say the words his father would have said, had he been here.

As he thought of the speech, still upstairs in his suitcase, the room began to spin. Melvin grasped the table top and held his breath. The first time it happened, the movement stopped, but within moments it returned. As shouts from his family rang out, Melvin collapsed to the floor of the restaurant, unconscious.

Melvin Moran was not a man given to fainting. It had never happened to him before, which is likely why his wife and family were so terrified to see him topple over. He was a man of tremendous energy. He had served in a top secret unit of the United States Air Force in England during the Korean War. He returned to the United States to work in his father's oil business, starting at the bottom with the roustabout crews and rising until he had taken over the business. He was involved in his community, serving as director and president of the Chamber of Commerce, the town's Industrial Foundation, and Rotary Club. He had served on the City Council, been elected mayor, named

Citizen of the Year, and inducted into his town's Hall of Fame. He was a director of the Oklahoma Independent Petroleum Association and served on his state's Academy for State Goals. He was a good husband and father and respected everywhere for his service to his synagogue, family, community, state, and his industry.

None of that mattered as he lay unconscious on the floor of a hotel in Jerusalem. Time seemed to stand still. Outside, the bustle of a busy city escalated as people started their workdays, the sun rose higher and grew warmer, the time for his speech drew nearer, and his family became more hysterical.

Within a few minutes, Melvin returned to consciousness. His family escorted him upstairs and put him into bed. A doctor was called. Melvin's temperature was 107 degrees. The doctor administered medication and Melvin was told to stay in bed.

Melvin would have moved heaven and earth to attend the ceremony, but his weakened condition made it clear that he was going nowhere.

"I guess you'll have to go on without me," he said sadly to Jasmine. "Take my speech from my suitcase. You'll have to read it in my place."

"We're not going anywhere," said his wife and daughter. "You're too sick to leave. We can get Sid to give the speech."

"No, please," Melvin said, weakly. "Do it for Dad."

Jasmine also had loved the old man. Now she was torn: whether to carry out her husband's wishes or to stay and take care of him. She had recalled Melvin with a high fever once before, during a family trip to Disneyland. He had been fine then…surely he would be this time, too.

CHAPTER TWO

Coming to America

"You may be the only Jewish person some of your classmates will ever meet. What they think about Jewish people is going to be what they think about you."
— Elsie Fine Moran

Meyer Moran, for whom the Ben-Gurion Library's wing is named, was of Spanish descent; he was born Meer Maron on August 13, 1903, in Resitza, Latvia. At the age of 18, his family set him aboard the SS *Latvia* to America to make his fortune. He left behind a brother and five sisters.

"Kohlberg, Kravis and Roberts Company [a private equity company] helped him come over," said Meyer's daughter, Jeannie Tiras, years later. "They were relatives of my grandfather. They lied about his age and said he was a year younger so he wouldn't have to go into the army.

"Here was this family telling this 18-year-old kid who doesn't speak English, 'Okay, you're going over and make money and bring us over.'"

Soon after Meer left, his father died. If he had died before Meer left Latvia, the young man might never have come to the United States; he would probably have had to stay in Latvia to help support the family. And with no one on the other side of the ocean to help them get out, the entire Maron family would likely have succumbed to the Nazis during World War II.

Not knowing a word of English, Meer made his way to Muncie, Indiana, where he worked for a short time for his uncle, George Roberts. He then moved on to Nowata, Oklahoma, where he had an uncle, Meyer Roberts.

Meer Americanized his own name and became Meyer Moran. He studied English at Nowata High School and worked for his uncle in the scrap iron business. In about 1924, Meyer moved to Maud and opened up his own scrap iron company and junkyard.

With no money and no credit, he took his hat in his hand and went to First National Bank in Seminole to ask for a loan. The banker, John Solomon, advanced Meyer $1,000, which he used to buy a pickup truck.

"Dad couldn't afford the truck and a place to live, so he lived and slept in the pickup," said his son, Melvin, years later. "He used the truck to purchase scrap from oilfield leases, which he then sold."

Elsie Fine and Meyer Moran met and married in 1929.

The bank's decision to take a chance on Meyer Moran made a great impact on the Latvian. He banked at First National in Seminole for the rest of his life, even long after he moved to Tulsa.

That level of dedication was a hallmark of Meyer Moran's life and a trait he passed on to his son.

Meyer had a friend who

worked for Phillips Petroleum Company and let him buy scrap from their wells. For the rest of his life, the only credit card Meyer ever used was a Phillips 66 card.

On a trip to Kansas City, Missouri, in 1929 Meyer met Elsie Fine, a secretary, on a blind date. He proposed on the third date and they were married in December, 1929.

The new Mrs. Moran had been born September 20, 1902, but where was subject to conjecture.

"She always told us that she was born in Poland," Melvin said. "One of her brothers told us later that she was born in Russia. And a sister told us she was born in Latvia."

Her family name was Fingerhut in Europe, but had been Americanized to Fine. The Fine family arrived at Ellis Island, New York, in 1906 on the SS *Pisa*. On the trip, the two younger sisters, Sara and Mary, took the measles and were quarantined upon arrival. While Elsie's two brothers and father left Ellis Island and traveled on to St. Joseph, the three girls and their mother stayed in quarantine. During this time of seclusion, Elsie's mother gave birth to her youngest son, David.

The Fine family, after finally arriving in St. Joseph, operated a small grocery store, and lived in two rooms of the same building. They had no indoor plumbing; later Elsie often told her children of the poverty in which she grew up. Seven people lived in two rooms. Several of the children slept on top of the piano.

Despite having left his family at a relatively young age, Meyer was very family oriented.

"Each time Dad earned enough money, he sent a ticket to Latvia for another member of his family to come over," Melvin said. "Eventually he brought his mother, his brother, and all of his sisters to America except for one. Her name was Sonia. He sent her a ticket, but World War II started and she was unable to come. She escaped the Holocaust by going to Siberia in Russia, where she spent the war years. After the war, she immigrated to Israel and lived there for the rest of her life.

"Dad was very hardworking, very charitable, and very patriotic," Melvin went on. "He understood that if America hadn't admitted him, he and all his family would have died during the Holocaust."

After their whirlwind courtship, Meyer and Elsie made their home at 203 Young Street in Maud, Oklahoma. In 1930 and again in 1932, Elsie returned to St. Joseph for the births of her sons, Melvin and Sidney. They lived in Maud until 1935, when they moved to Seminole.

The junk yard business had become Moran Pipe and Supply, which sold mostly used oilfield equipment. Two years after moving to Seminole, Meyer purchased his first oil well; it was the beginning of Moran Oil Company.

"We first lived on Wilson Street," Melvin said. "But the first home I can remember was on the southeast corner of Seminole and University."

Life in the Moran household was peaceful. "I cannot recall, during my entire lifetime, a single harsh word

Melvin Moran was born September 18, 1930, in St. Joseph, Missouri.

between any of us," Melvin said. "We have always been cheer-leaders for each other."

For as long as Elsie and Meyer Moran lived, their home was kosher. Eating kosher foods means that Jews eat only the meat of clean, or kosher, animals, as outlined in the Bible. Their beef, turkey, chicken, lamb, and venison are cleaned of fat, drained of blood, and well-cooked. They do not eat pork or shellfish. But "keeping kosher" was not an easy thing to do in 1930's Seminole.

"We had to get our meat from a kosher butcher shop in Tulsa," Melvin remembered. "But it was very important to my parents to be a good representation of their religion. I remember my mother saying to me one day, 'Melvin, you are the only Jewish child in your class and you may be the only Jewish person some of your classmates will ever meet. So what they think about Jewish people is going to be what they think about you. You have to be good for that reason.'"

Melvin's brother, Sidney, remembers Maud almost better than Seminole. He was three when the family moved to Seminole, two years younger than Melvin. "We had a brick house with chickens in the back yard. I remember feeding them," Sidney said.

"We kept them for the eggs," Melvin said. "Not for the meat, because we kept a kosher home."

"In Seminole, we had a little wood-frame house. I once tried to locate it, but every house looked the same," Sid said.

Sid remembers his brother as a child much the same as he is as a man. "Mel was very protective, energetic, and dynamic, even as a kid," Sid said. "He protected me from bullies, included

Melvin Moran grew up in Maud and Seminole, moving to Tulsa in the seventh grade.

me in his circle of friends and games."
He said Melvin was a very fine
scholar. "In Seminole, there was only
one teacher per class and the teachers
always remembered him and encouraged me to be like him," Sid said. "He
was a great big brother. I don't remember fighting, just encour-
agement. He was a tremendous pal to me. Nobody could ask
for a better big brother."

Melvin may have gotten his dynamic personality from his
father. Meyer was high energy, like Mel and Jeannie, according
to Sid.

"My mother was more wise," Sid remembered. "My teen
friends came to her for advice. My earliest childhood recol-
lection was when I was maybe two or three years old, before I
could read. She would sit with me with *The Book of Knowledge*
and show me pictures of mountains, planets, and stars and talk
about how far the sky goes. She was wonderful at stimulating
us. I was wide-eyed. It made me want to read and I did at a
fairly early age."

Melvin strives to be soft spoken like his mother and charitable like his father.

"I feel I am patriotic like my father and my father was also
extremely charitable," he said. "I try to follow that because he
was never a wealthy person, and during the early days, he was
an extremely poor person. But no matter what he had, he was

always charitable and he taught us that from the very beginning."

Melvin reciprocated the respect he got from his younger brother.

"My brother, Sidney, was and is extremely intelligent," he said. "When I was 14, I was reading comic books. When Sid was 14, he was reading Einstein." In one of Einstein's books, Sid found what he thought was an error in Albert Einstein's thinking. So he wrote to Einstein and told him so. He received a response from Einstein, saying, "What I wrote was true. But what you said was equally true." Sid's photo and story was carried by Associated Press all over the country with the headline "Tulsa 14-Year-Old Boy Gets Draw with Einstein."

"Our father started with absolute zero and became very successful," Sid said. "Neither of our parents had a college education, but there was never any question that we'd have one. When I was small, I asked Mom how long was school and she said 12 years and then college. I never knew college wasn't a requirement."

Melvin had lots of friends in 1930's Seminole, but his three closest friends were Joe Snider, Robert Hammons, and Donna Pollock. All three were a year ahead of him in school. They played together almost every day, either in the Moran home or in their homes or out in the street.

"I believe I am Melvin's oldest living friend," said Donna Pollock Terry. "He moved into our neighborhood three houses down from me and two houses down from Joe Snider.

"The town was highly segregated. Blacks lived across the tracks and worked for us for a pittance. They even had their own fountains. At that time, there were no Jews in Seminole and I'm ashamed of how the Moran family was treated.

"But we were little kids and his coming opened up exciting new ways of life to us," Terry continued. "We never knew about Jews. Melvin had curly black hair and a lisp; I'd never heard a lisp before.

"When we went to his house, the food smelled different, his father wore one of those little skull caps. If Joe invited him for lunch, Melvin couldn't come because he didn't eat our kind of food. He didn't go to our churches."

The friends joined the school's foreign stamp club. "Mrs. Buxton was our collection teacher," Terry said. "She showed us there was another world out there."

Terry remembers one afternoon with Melvin and his cousin, Iris. "Melvin's father had been instrumental in bringing Iris, her mother, and cousin out of Latvia just before everyone there was going to the concentration camps," Terry said. "Melvin brought her to play with us, but she only spoke Latvian. She had blond hair that she wore in braids. I wanted to know her and we tried to communicate with her by shouting. She did pick up English quickly."

One of the friends' favorite pastimes was the serial movies at the Rex or State theaters on Saturday afternoon, especially during the summertime.

"Iris hadn't mastered English yet when we went to a show about a dog, called 'The Chicken Eater,'" Terry said. "Another family accused the dog of eating their chickens, but the dog's family knew she hadn't. In the movie you got to know the dog and like her and then they'd killed her because she was supposed to be a chicken eater.

"I remember she left a lot of puppies. We were all so sad because the dog died. We all cried. We left the theater all sniffling and holding hands.

"It was a hot day and I remember thinking that, although Iris didn't understand the English, she understood what had happened, and in our sadness, we were all communicating. All that sadness opened up an understanding that I treasured, like the first communication of children.

"I'm still friends with Iris today; she lives in Florida."

Although Melvin and Terry lost touch when both moved from Seminole, they were reunited 50 years later and are still close today, meeting and traveling together frequently with their spouses.

Joe Snider, Melvin's other childhood friend, was active in the speech and debate program at Seminole High School, taught by the legendary H.B. Mitchell. He was Seminole's first national champion in speech. He later became a lawyer and was a founding member of Oklahoma City's most prominent law firms, Fellers-Snider. He and Melvin stayed close until his death.

The third of Melvin's friends, Robert Hammons, also went through the Seminole High School speech and debate program and became a prominent Baptist minister. He spent many years as pastor of First Baptist Church in Seminole, becoming as beloved and respected a member of the community as Melvin himself.

Melvin attended first grade in Seminole and remained in Seminole until the second semester of seventh grade.

"When G-d passed out talent in music and art, I was bypassed completely," Melvin said, laughing over those years at Seminole elementary schools, and refraining from speaking or spelling the name of God, as is his custom and the custom of most devout Jews.

When he was seven or eight, his mother wanted Melvin to learn to play the violin. He took one violin lesson. At the end of the lesson, the teacher said, "Mrs. Moran, if you want to go ahead and waste your money, that's fine with me, but there is no hope for him."

Then Melvin was introduced to tap dancing.

"If I say so myself, I thought I was pretty accomplished," Melvin said. "I loved the recitals. I kept all my costumes. One year I was a pirate. Another year I was a sailor. Another year I was a soldier."

BELOW: Meyer Moran's business expanded from a junk shop in Maud to pipe and supply businesses in Seminole, and Kamay, Texas, during the early 1940s.

Meyer Moran and his children in 1938.

Years later, long after Melvin was married and moved back to Seminole, he and his dad were talking about his days of tap dancing. "Mel, I went to all your recitals, but I was so ashamed," Meyer said. "Apparently I was so bad!" Melvin laughed.

The Moran family moved to Tulsa in late 1941, Meyer leaving his sister's husband as a partner to run his Seminole office. Melvin stayed with George and Ella Kahn to finish his first semester, then rejoined his family in January.

"We moved to Tulsa when I was nine so my brother could begin bar mitzvah training, which we couldn't get in Seminole," Sid said. "Dad moved for our benefit."

Bar mitzvah is the coming of age of young Jewish men, similar to confirmation in the Christian religion.

"It's where you begin to take responsibility for your own actions and life," Sid explained. "It's when you become a young adult and are accepted into the Jewish community: today I am a man. To prepare, you learn to read Hebrew, recite prayers, and lead an adult congregation. You learn Jewish history and ethics and what our religion is about. You learn to read the Torah. The ceremony is very impressive to a boy of 13. It takes a year and a half or two years to prepare. It's a big deal."

Melvin's "baby sister" Jeannie was born four years after Sid.

"I remember attending nursery school in Seminole, but we moved to Tulsa when I was four or five," she said.

"I remember the two-story brick house we lived in on Cincinnati Street. There was always someone living with us — cousins, uncles, or aunts. I had a room of my own, but I always shared it with somebody. My brothers shared a room.

Melvin's entire extended family sat for a portrait in their Tulsa living room in 1942.

People came and went all the time. My father was always helping people who needed a place to stay. My grandmother, Minnie Moran, lived with us until she died. She had the room next to mine."

Melvin remembers his parents taking in soldiers during the war. "My parents were very religious and they would go to the synagogue on Friday nights," he said. "There would always be soldiers there from Camp Gruber in Muskogee. My parents would always bring them home for the weekend so they'd have family."

To Melvin, his mother was the gentlest person on earth and instilled in him and his siblings some very important lessons.

"My mother didn't drive, so after we moved to Tulsa, if my father was not available to take her, we traveled by bus," Melvin said. "Those were days of segregation. There was a sign in the front of the bus which read 'Colored People Use Rear Seat.'

"My mother was infuriated by that. When we would take the bus, we [led by my mother] would always sit in the rear seat with the African American riders. We would do that no matter how many seats were empty at the front of the bus. If the back seat was full, then African American riders would have to stand. In those instances, we always stood with them.

Melvin attended Horace Mann Junior High during the 1940s.

"Mother was the first civil rights activist that I had ever seen. She taught us a wonderful lesson. She was the most gentle person I ever knew and this was her way of protesting this terrible injustice."

Melvin went away to college when Jeannie was only 10 so her early memories of him were sketchy.

"I remember the marble races in our driveway," she said. "Kids came from all over, but Mel would always win. It was during the war and we didn't have a lot of toys. We literally had an open house – his friends were always over."

She remembers Melvin's paper route — he used to wrap his newspapers in the kitchen. "He always worked," she said. "Both my brothers did."

Melvin's first job was delivering the *Tulsa Tribune*. "I loved it," he said. His paper route was in the area of the Philbrook Museum of Art. In fact, the Philbrook was one of his customers. On most of his route were big, beautiful homes — generally one home to a block. "It never occurred to me that if I delivered papers on a block with 10 homes, that I would make 10 times as much money," Melvin said.

He delivered newspapers by bicycle, throwing them as he drove by. Each week that the carriers didn't receive a "kick," or complaint, they would get a free movie pass, and Melvin loved the movies.

"Sometimes my aim wasn't very good as I delivered to some of the smaller homes," Melvin said. "I would accidentally throw the paper on the roof. When I did that, I would be a paper short. And I never wanted to be a paper short, because invariably I would get a kick." So, since the newspaper usually had several sections, Melvin laid half of a newspaper flat on the front lawn of one home and the other half flat on the front lawn of another home. "That way one newspaper would take care of two homes, I thought, and I wouldn't get a kick," Melvin said. "My thinking was that the homeowner would think that the other half of his newspaper had simply blown away."

Melvin tried to put the halves on lawns at least a block apart, but one day he forgot he was a paper short. "I had two homes to go on my route and only one paper," he said. "So I did my little trick on two homes adjoining each other.

"Bad mistake! That evening I went by to collect and when I got to one of those homes, the owner said to me, 'Normally I would not mind going next door to read the other half of my paper. But my neighbor and I are not speaking so I couldn't do that.'

"I still kept doing my little thing, but I was always careful and put the one half of the newspaper on a lawn that was not adjacent to the home which was the recipient of the other half."

Years later, when Melvin was driving through his old neighborhood with his 12-year-old son, Melvin told him about his job delivering newspapers.

As they were driving around, Melvin remembered an incident from those years. "I stopped the car and said to David, 'See that house up on the hill? In that house used to live the biggest, meanest dog in Tulsa." Melvin told how the dog rushed him and he was afraid it was going to chew his leg off. He took a rolled-up newspaper and tried to hit him on the head with it. The dog opened up his huge jaws, clamped down on the newspaper, and walked docilely away. The next day, the same thing happened. So for the next several years, Melvin ordered one extra newspaper for the dog. It cost him five cents a day, but he was never bitten.

"That was the best investment I have ever made," Melvin said, in telling the story to his son.

David responded with, "Dad, why didn't you give the dog yesterday's paper?"

"That had never occurred to me," Melvin said.

Melvin's next job was working at Page Drug Store, located at the corner of 18th Street and Cincinnati.

"I was so pleased to get that job that I did not ask what my pay would be and I did not find out until the following week," Melvin said.

"I worked eight hours a day, seven days a week. My total

salary, before Social Security deductions, was $12. It worked out to about 16 cents an hour. I really felt I was worth $20. Mr. Page did tell me that I could help myself to a drink if I was thirsty. So I decided that I would receive my $20 a week by helping myself to milkshakes. Well, I gained a lot of weight — so much so that Mr. Page offered me a longer lunch hour."

Melvin next went to work at Crawford's Drug Store at 21st and Utica. Because he was now an "experienced" soda jerk, he earned his $20 a week; he worked there for two summers.

Life in the Morans' Tulsa household was not always quiet, Jeannie remembered.

"Our father wasn't at home much when I was growing up and I don't think Mel and Sid had much more of his time than I did," she said. "He was always out in the field, but whenever he was home, you knew it. He was not quiet. He was a very strong character. He and I had plenty of tiffs. He was not easy to communicate with. I was probably more like him than my mother.

"I would go to his office and it would be full of all these maps. He'd say this well was a dry hole and this well was a dry hole. He'd never talk about his successes. I'd say, 'Daddy, if all these are dry holes, how do we live?'"

In the 1970s, Jeannie wanted to go into business with some friends. Banks did not want to loan money to women back then, so she went to her father and asked for a loan. "Absolutely not!" he said. "You'd be bankrupt in no time!"

"We finally did get the money and I spent my life trying to prove he was wrong," Jeannie said. "He finally admitted it, but he was from the European culture at a time when women didn't work — they should be in the kitchen."

Melvin attended Horace Mann Junior High and then graduated from Tulsa Central in 1947.

"In high school Melvin won awards for the best everything," Sid said.

Mel remembers it differently. "I loved to sing," he said. "In eighth grade, I enrolled in a class of choral music. And I remember the teacher's name — Mrs. Cook. Well, at the end of the very first class, the bell rang and Mrs. Cook said, 'Will Melvin Moran remain in the classroom please?'

"After everyone had exited, Mrs. Cook said to me, 'Melvin, if you would like to pass this course, I would like for you to use this hour as a study hour. Your voice is ruining the entire class.'

"So I did."

Tulsa schools were very different than Seminole schools. Melvin's graduating class at Tulsa Central had 1,000 students.

At Tulsa Central, Melvin ran with several other Jewish boys.

"My two closest friends were Mervin Aptak and Maynard Ungerman," Melvin recalled. "My next two closest friends were Marvin Lebow and Melvin Feldman. We were sometimes referred to as the Five Ms."

"Melvin and I have been friends since 1945," said Aptak. "We went to the same high school and were classmates in some classes. I remember in physics, one of our assignments was to draw a diagram of a radio. Melvin's drawing was so bad, the teacher wrote, 'I don't know what you have here' but gave him a good grade anyway.

"We had wonderful times," Aptak said. "We all had relatives in Kansas City, so we'd go there on vacations. Melvin was excellent about finding his way around there. As soon as we'd come back to Tulsa, he'd be totally lost."

The "Ms" took the train and stayed with relatives, spending their time visiting other teens, "usually girls," said Maynard Ungerman.

"We would hang out at Plaza Square, which is like the Utica Square of Kansas City," Ungerman said. "And we loved a barbecue place there. Once we took a trip to Houston and found barbecue sandwiches for five cents each. I'm still looking for that place when I'm in Houston."

"Melvin was never into mischief like we were, though," Aptak said. "I never heard Melvin say anything bad about anybody. If he thought anything bad, he'd be quiet or find something positive to say to counteract it. Even in high school. Melvin does not change; [as an adult] he's the same Melvin as in high school."

In those days, double- and triple-dating was popular, Aptak remembered. "Whoever could get their dad's car would drive. Melvin was a year younger than me, so he had to ride with Maynard or me most of the time," he said.

Ungerman attended a different Tulsa high school, but knew Melvin and Mervin from the Jewish boys' organization, AZA.

"I might have known Melvin from Hebrew school, too, but I didn't pay attention there," Ungerman said. "I hated Hebrew school. In those days, and this was 65 years ago, the teachers' idea was that if you didn't get it, they would hit you over the head with a ruler. They'd hire any Orthodox Jew who came from Europe to be a teacher at Hebrew School, just because he was an Orthodox Jew from Europe. Not many of us learned very much from them."

The boys would visit Melvin when he worked at the soda shop. "Most of us didn't want to work," Ungerman said. "Oh, we'd say we were working for our fathers and some of us did work a few hours a week. Melvin really did work."

Ungerman dated Mel's cousin, George Kahn's daughter, Iris, for awhile. "We did typical, silly kid stuff," Ungerman said. "I remember once we stayed out all night. We parked in Mel's driveway. I was with Iris. I can't remember who he was with."

During his high school years, Melvin dated a lot, but only had one crush.

"Her name was Laverne Smith," Melvin said. "There were many very pretty girls in my class. Laverne was gorgeous. I had wanted to ask her out on a date for a long time, but it took me months to get up the nerve. She said no. I was crushed."

Her rejection may have had something to do with the fact that Melvin was only 16 when he graduated from high school; Smith would have been a year or two older than him.

During high school, Melvin's synagogue had a team in the church basketball league and Melvin signed up. The games were played on a high school court several miles from Melvin's home. The team members would pick each other up to drive to games.

Although Melvin loved basketball, he was not very good. He played for several years and his high score during a game was two points — he made two free throws and was "so proud."

The day after his 16th birthday, Melvin obtained his driver's license. He was already a senior in high school. They had a basketball game that week, so he called several of the players and offered to pick them up. He picked up four players and headed to the gym, but it was Melvin's first time to take the car without his father. "I drove very cautiously and very, very slowly," Melvin said. "I am not certain that I ever reached the speed of 20 miles per hour.

"My friends urged me to go faster, but I declined to do so. We finally reached the site about 30 minutes after the scheduled time for the game. The referee had declared a forfeit on our part and the other team had already gone home. That was the last time I drove my teammates to the game."

In high school, Melvin wrote for the school paper, *School Life*, and already his talent for comedy was becoming well known. Without his knowledge, a teacher entered copies of his humor column in a national contest and he won first place.

"That made me think that perhaps I had some ability in humor writing," Melvin said. "So I decided that I wanted to become a writer of comedy for television. I had heard that the University of Missouri in Columbia had an excellent School of Journalism, so that is where I attended college."

Funny things happen to Melvin Moran. Whether he became interested in comedy because he had a talent for it, or because humor just had a way of finding him wherever he was, is not clear. But even by this time of Melvin's life, he began to develop the dry wit and the impeccable timing of a professional comedian.

"In the summer of 1945, my family and I were going to Colorado for our summer vacation," Melvin said. "We were

Melvin graduated from Tulsa Central in 1947.

in the Pike's Peak/Manitou Springs area visiting some friends, former Seminole veterinarian Dr. Jack Winters and his family.

"We had been sightseeing all day and, as evening approached, we looked for a place for dinner. It was tourist season and none of the restaurants we tried could take nine more people. One of the restaurant owners suggested that we try a restaurant located part of the way up the mountain."

They drove to the Swiss-style cottage, which had been converted into a restaurant. There were quite a few cars around and they all wondered if the restaurant was full.

"I suggested that everyone remain in their cars while I checked inside," Melvin said. "As I walked up on the porch, there was a woman seated in front of a small table. I assumed that she had something to do with crowd control. I asked, 'Are you full?'

"She answered yes. As I started to walk back to the car, she yelled after me, 'I assume you are asking about the condition of my stomach. I have just eaten here and am indeed full. If you are asking about the capacity of the restaurant, I have no idea.'

"As it turned out, there was plenty of room inside and we had a lovely dinner."

As a graduation present, the Morans gave Melvin a trip to New York. He invited his two high school friends and younger brother Sid to accompany him.

"After being in New York for a couple of days, I decided I needed a haircut," Melvin said. "I walked by a barbershop near the hotel and haircuts were advertised for 75 cents. In Tulsa at that time they were $1, so I thought, 'Things are really not that expensive in New York after all.'"

It was a small shop with only two chairs, so Melvin and his brother sat down.

"My barber was a very nice middle-aged man," Melvin remembered. "He kept asking, 'Your first trip to New York, huh? You enjoying our city? We hope you are.' What a nice man, I kept thinking.

"The barber put something in my hair and rubbed my head for about 20 seconds," Melvin continued. "It felt good. 'What a nice man,' I thought. And then he put some cream on my face and quickly wiped it off. Again, I thought how kind he was. While this was going on, I noticed that my brother was having the same stuff put on his hair and on his face.

"Our entire time in the barber chair probably lasted only three or four minutes. But after all, what could I expect for 75 cents? Then he handed us the bill. It was about $10 each. Whatever he put into my hair was a Brazilian shampoo and whatever he put on my face was an African facial."

Melvin's next trip was years later. "I made it a point to walk by that barber shop to see if it still existed," Melvin said. "It did. And as I walked by, I noticed a man in the barber shop with cream on his face."

After their expensive haircuts and other expensive pur-
chases, Melvin and his friends needed to save whatever money
they could. In the newspaper they read ads for air trips from
New York to Los Angeles that seemed incredibly cheap.

"The trips were on non-scheduled airlines," Melvin said.
"So we went to the non-scheduled airline office. We asked if
they had any planes stopping in Tulsa. The airline employee
asked how many of us there were. We said four. They said,
'We'll stop.'

"And they did. As I recall, I think it was about 3:00 a.m....
but we saved money!"

Meyer Moran had been sent to the United States on his
own at 18 and believed his son should also be independent.

"I went to college when I was 16," Melvin said. "I enrolled
by mail, so I had never been to Columbia when I arrived there
to begin my college courses. Mom and Dad put me on a bus in
Tulsa and, in effect, said, 'Go and get an education.'"

In those days college was pretty cheap. Out-of-state tuition
for Melvin's first semester was $50.

Melvin decided that he would like to join a fraternity. He
received invitations to visit the three Jewish fraternities. Since
he was only 16 and planning to live in a fraternity house for
the new four years, Melvin wondered how to choose "the best
fraternity brothers possible."

Melvin arrived in Columbia early in the evening just before rush week began. "I don't remember if I checked into a hotel or a dormitory for the night," he said. "But as I had nothing
else to do, I thought it would be helpful for me to locate where
the three fraternity houses were because I would be making

repeated visits to those houses beginning the next morning."

He walked over to the first house. The fraternity brothers were busy getting ready. Some were on ladders painting, some were sweeping, and some were cleaning. Melvin walked into the house and some of them said "hi." He said "hi" and that was the extent of the conversation.

At the second house, everything was repeated. Again, there were a few 'hi's' and that was about it.

"Finally I walked into the third fraternity house, Sigma Alpha Mu," Melvin remembered. "Again the guys were painting, sweeping, and cleaning. But as I walked into the house, things were quite different there. Everyone came down from their ladders, laid down their brooms, put away their cleaning rags and everyone came over to me and began visiting with me. They

Melvin and his friends register for a Sigma Alpha Mu conference in Winnipeg in 1946.

asked where I was from, why I selected the University of Missouri, what would be my major. Everyone was so friendly.

"On the spot, I made up my mind these were the fellows I would want to live with for the next four years."

Rush Week began and for the next three days, Melvin visited all three houses several times. During Rush Week, everyone was friendly, but he already had made up his mind.

"At the end of Rush Week, all three fraternities invited me to join," Melvin said. "And I joined Sigma Alpha Mu. I had four wonderful happy years there. Several years later, I was elected president."

Months later, Melvin found out why one group was so friendly compared to the others. During the six months they were pledging the fraternity, one requirement was to meet and greet everybody who walked into the fraternity house. And on Monday nights, they were questioned to be certain they had fulfilled this requirement. After Melvin was initiated into the fraternity six months later, meeting and greeting was no longer a requirement. But the new pledges were so used to jumping up and meeting everyone that almost all of them continued the practice throughout four years of college.

In later life, Melvin's practice of "meeting and greeting" became a common thread, one he reiterated to his fellow civic club members whenever he got the chance.

At 16, Melvin was the youngest of the fraternity brothers, which often caused him embarrassing moments.

One afternoon when the phone rang, whoever answered yelled out, "It's for Moran!" Someone else yelled back, "He's in the bathroom — pretending to shave!"

Melvin never forgot an embarrassing weekend visit to St. Louis in 1949. "Does anyone remember which way car doors opened in 1949?" he asked, smiling. "I do. And I shall never forget. One weekend a fraternity brother invited me to come home with him to St. Louis for the weekend. I was in the back seat. It was very cold and I was wearing an overcoat. As we were driving down the highway at about 60 or 70 miles per hour, I noticed that my coat was caught in the door. I didn't want to bother the driver. I thought I would simply open the door an inch, pull my coat in and then shut the door.

"In those days, rear car doors opened just the opposite of the way they do now. So when I opened the door just slightly, the wind caught the door and pulled it off its hinges. For obvious reasons, that was the last time I was invited to St. Louis for the weekend."

At Columbia, Melvin began taking pre-journalism classes right away. During his sophomore year, an instructor told his class that a beginning writer could probably start at $25 a week.

"I decided that there must be something better than that," Melvin said. The next day he switched out of journalism and into the business school. "I never regretted making that decision," he said.

In college, Melvin said he dated quite a lot, but had only one crush.

"Her name was Karla Samuelson," he said. "She lived in Kansas City." Samuelson graduated high school two years after Melvin. Whenever he could, he would spend weekends in Kansas City. When Samuelson graduated high school, to

Melvin's dismay, she chose the University of Oklahoma for her college studies. Melvin immediately told his mother he wanted to transfer to OU.

"My mother said, 'No, if something is meant to happen, it will. You should stay where you are,'" Melvin said "It was wonderful advice."

But Melvin continued to write to Samuelson at OU.

"During Christmas break, I hoped to take her out on New Year's Eve," Melvin said. "I remember trying to be clever. There

Melvin's parents in the 1950s.

Melvin, center, with his brother, Sidney, and sister, Jeannie, in 1951.

was a new song out called, 'What Are You Doing New Year's Eve.' I bought the record and sent it to her. Not long afterwards, I received a 'Dear John' letter from Karla advising me that she had become engaged to an OU student from Ardmore.

"Receiving that letter was a devastating experience," Melvin said. He later met the Ardmore student, who he found to be a fine young man. Samuelson married him and they moved to Dallas, where her husband headed a major advertising firm.

Before Melvin graduated from college, his old high school friend, Maynard Ungerman, invited Melvin to his wedding. The wedding was held in the Beverly Hills Hotel in California.

"This was a very fancy hotel," Melvin remembered of the trip. There was an outdoor swimming pool and near the pool there was a table tennis table. Guests were playing table tennis, with the winner staying on and taking challenges from other guests. When it came Melvin's turn to challenge, he won the match and beat a number of guests afterwards.

"Finally a short fellow about 10 years older than I was challenged me," Melvin said. "He said, 'how about playing for a malt?' and I said sure. We had a very close game and, as I recall, he defeated me 21-19."

Melvin again was challenged to play, this time each player put up a dollar. "Again I accepted the challenge," Melvin said. "This time, he absolutely killed me. I don't remember the exact score, but it was something like 21-5."

As Melvin was leaving, someone asked him if he knew who he had been playing. He learned the man was Bobby Riggs, who, at the time, was the table tennis champion of California.

Riggs was also a professional tennis champion and most famous for the match he played against female tennis star Billie Jean King.

"Even in his younger days, he was hustling people," Melvin said. "But for the dollar, it was well worth it!"

Later, during his military career, Melvin played championship table tennis all over England and still was winning matches in his 70s.

During his college summers, Melvin went home to Tulsa and worked downtown in the menswear department at Streets Department Store. Melvin found humor even at work.

"One day a woman came in and said she was interested in looking at a short-sleeved shirt," Melvin said. "I misunderstood her and thought she said shorts. I asked the routine questions: white or colored?"

"White," she said.

"Cotton or cotton knit?"

"Cotton," she replied.

"Would you be interested in the boxer style?"

"I don't know what that is, but can my husband wear it outside of his pants?" she asked, perplexed.

"Well, he can wear it anywhere he wishes, but customarily, it is worn under the pants," Melvin said, bringing out a pair of boxer shorts. It was then that he understood that she wanted a shirt.

Another time he was showing clothing to a woman who looked very familiar. "I had no idea who she was, but she mentioned recently seeing my mother," Melvin said. "Then she said she played bridge with my Aunt Sylvia and mentioned several other relatives of mine, so it was obviously someone I should have known.

"I was hoping not to embarrass myself by letting her know that I didn't know her name. I hoped she wouldn't buy anything, but she did. Then I was hoping she'd pay with cash, but she didn't.

" 'Charge it,' she said.

"I had only one more opportunity to escape embarrassment," Melvin remembered. " 'Now how do you spell your last name?' I asked. She responded, 'S-M-I-T-H.'"

Although he had never been a professional comedian, Melvin still loved performing. Always the optimist, he tried singing again in college.

Melvin attended the University of Missouri, graduating in 1951 with a master's degree in business administration.

"My college fraternity had a choir and we would do serenades," he said. "At the beginning of my first year in college, the choir director asked for volunteers who would like to sing. Of course, I volunteered. Most of the people volunteering auditioned, but when the director asked what range my voice was, I answered, 'bass.' Well, he was short of men in the bass section, so I was able to participate without the audition.

"At the end of our first serenade, the director came to me and said, 'Would you like to remain in the choir?' I said 'Yes, I would.' He said, 'If you want to remain, you may move your mouth and pretend to sing, but I do not want to hear any sound from you.' And I did that."

But Melvin Moran loved the arts and later married a professional singer, dancer, and actress. He may have been rejected by his violin teacher, by his father as a tap dancer, by Mrs. Cook and the college choir director as a singer, but he later was proud to be appointed to the Oklahoma Arts Council by Oklahoma Governor Frank Keating. He has spent much of his life contributing to the arts.

Melvin, interested in comedy from an early age, dressed as Raggedy Andy for a costume party during his years at the University of Missouri.

CHAPTER THREE

Jasmine in Jerusalem

"I guess it was just ordained by God."

— Jasmine Moran

The temperature in Jerusalem that December day reached into the mid 50s as Jasmine and Marilyn reluctantly left Melvin alone in his hotel room, but not before fussing over him. His wife pressed a cool cloth to his forehead and he closed his eyes. The chill of the wet fabric felt wonderful to his fevered brow. The room darkened as Jasmine pulled the blinds. Immediately the room felt cooler.

He could feel his own heat against the sheets and the light blanket they had pulled over him. His whole body reverberated with the beat of his heart, pounding hard against his chest as his body struggled to deal with the intense fever. Weakness like he had never experienced made his limbs heavy and all he could do was lay still.

Jasmine stood near the bed watching him for several minutes. She could see how sick he was. Married for nearly 30 years, there was not much about her husband that she did not know or intuit and she knew now that her husband was very ill. Only a very important event such as today's dedication could have drawn her from his side. And even that would not have, if it had not meant so much to Melvin for her to go.

In fact, Jasmine did not feel much better than Melvin. It only had been a few weeks since she had undergone a radical hysterectomy. For weeks she had been so weak she could barely think of the long trip to Israel. It was for this reason that she had insisted that Marilyn accompany them. Although she would have preferred to stay at home to recuperate, it meant so much to Melvin for her to be here today.

He was such a strong person, she thought, looking down on her husband. You might not guess it to look at him. He was still small, much like the "97-pound weakling" she joked that he was when they met in 1952 in London. They had been through so much together. He had courted her, won her, and moved her across the ocean, away from all of her family and friends. Together they had relocated from the metropolis of London where she had been a West End showgirl to the small town of Seminole, Oklahoma. She hated Seminole at first, crying every night about the lack of amenities, the Midwestern heat, and the hard work of homemaking, all new to her. And Melvin had tried hard to make her happy, driving on weekends to Oklahoma City or Tulsa for the theater or symphony. She came to rely on him so much over the years. Melvin had shown himself to be strong and reliable, funny and quick, a good husband and father.

She could not let him down now. Despite her worst fears about his health, Jasmine knew she had to go to the dedication. Making sure her husband was comfortable, she drew her daughter out the door to rejoin the rest of their family. The show, after all, must go on.

CHAPTER FOUR

Coming of Age

"It would be accurate to say that I met Jasmine as a result of my encounter with a car thief."

— Melvin Moran

Melvin received his bachelor's degree in business administration from the University of Missouri in 1951, the same week his younger brother graduated from the University of Texas at age 20 with a master's degree.

Melvin had taken AIR-ROTC in college, so he was commissioned as a second lieutenant upon his graduation. He was assigned to the 8th Air Force Depot Squadron (AFDS), at first as an air police officer at Sandia Base in Albuquerque, New Mexico. The unit's job was loading and unloading atomic weapons.

"That assignment lasted only briefly," Melvin said. "I was assigned as a supply officer and scheduled to go to supply school. Then very suddenly my orders were changed and my squadron was ordered to go to England."

Melvin during his Air Force career.

There were many things to do before he went. "We had a checklist of things to do," Melvin recalled. "One was to get certain shots. Another was to qualify on the gun range with a carbine and a pistol. Guns have never been my thing and when I went out to the range to qualify, that was the first time I ever fired a gun. But it seemed pretty simple. I had watched people fire guns in the movies for years."

A perfect score would be 100; 70 was passing. "I think the lowest score ever recorded was somewhere around 40 and, if I recall correctly, my score was about 20," Melvin said. "Obviously I failed — big time. So I was ordered to try again a week later."

During that week Melvin had no instruction and did not touch a gun again until he returned to the firing range. Under the direction of a Sergeant Rosenberg, however, this time Melvin scored in the upper 80s.

Years later, Melvin learned what everyone else in his squadron already knew. Whenever Melvin shot, Rosenberg fired at the same target. "He is the one who caused me to qualify on the gun range and that allowed me to be shipped to England with my squadron," Melvin said, an event that shaped Melvin's entire life.

Ironically, Melvin also was able later to help Sergeant Rosenberg. By then he was stationed at Lakenheath Base in England, 70 miles north of London and 20 miles from Cambridge. One day Melvin's commanding officer, Major Kerner, ordered Melvin to his office. "Sergeant Rosenberg was an air police sergeant in our squadron," Melvin recalled. "Major Kerner informed me that the night before Sergeant Rosenberg had gotten drunk and slugged one of our officers."

The major said, "Normally I would throw Sergeant

Rosenberg into the brig and throw away the key. But I really like you, Lieutenant Moran, and I don't want you to think that I am anti-Semitic. So instead of doing that, I am going to transfer him from air police into your supply section. I want you to be responsible for him."

"So I was," Melvin said. "And he was one of the best airmen I had in my section."

There were about 225 men in Melvin's squadron, including 25 officers. Except for three persons, the squadron went to England by ship. The captain in charge of the technical areas, a sergeant in charge of the air police, and Melvin were ordered to England by air ahead of the rest of the squadron to prepare the way.

"Keep in mind that, at that point, I had had no supply training whatsoever," Melvin said. "I was given a loose-leaf supply requisition book approximately a foot thick with instructions about how to requisition everything from guns to typewriters to bedding. I was ordered to read the book on the trip so that I could have things ready for everyone when they arrived."

The plan was for the three officers to fly from Sandia Base to Kilmer Base in New Jersey and from there to Lakenheath Base, where they would be located for the next two years.

They flew to Kilmer to catch a flight on a military plane. But at that time, there was a plane lost over the Atlantic and all available planes were searching for survivors. The officers were told that no one knew exactly what day there would be a plane to fly them to England. "The captain and I stayed in the officers' quarters while the sergeant stayed in quarters for non-commissioned officers," Melvin said.

Every morning at 8:00 a.m., they were to call a phone number and find out if there would be a plane that day. If not, they were free to do whatever they wished.

For the next several days, they made the phone call every morning and were told there were no planes available. Then one day Melvin and the captain took a train into New York City and spent the day there, taking the train back in the evening. After taking the train back and forth for several days, Melvin suggested that they could stay over in New York City, get up early and make the phone call from there.

"If our plane was leaving that day, we could fairly quickly catch the train back to Kilmer," Melvin said. "If not, we could stay in New York, having saved the trip back and forth."

On the fourth day, they met some people and partied until late. The next morning they overslept. When they made the call to Kilmer, they were informed that their plane already had taken off.

The sergeant accompanying Melvin and the captain had made his morning call and met the flight. However, he chose not to board at the last minute when Melvin and the captain did not arrive.

"The captain was carrying some top-secret papers," Melvin said. "An armed courier was to meet the plane to secure the papers and deliver them elsewhere. We were lucky we were not court-martialed when the plane landed without us." They caught a plane for England the following day.

Upon arrival in England, Melvin and his cohorts were driven to Lakenheath.

"With help, I was able to requisition everything that I was

supposed to," Melvin said. "The rest of the squadron arrived several weeks later."

The squadron's job was loading and unloading atomic weapons. "It was a very technical process," Melvin said. "But my job was in supply, so I wasn't very involved in that."

There was not enough room for the entire squadron in the living quarters on the base, so some, including Melvin, were required to live off base.

"I found a room in an English boarding house in Exning, a suburb of Newmarket, a famous horseracing city about 20 miles from the base," Melvin said.

Melvin's first roommate was fellow officer Bob Scholtens, who later married an English woman and moved out. His second roommate was fellow officer Ray Lavendar, a married man whose wife did not come to England. Following release from the service, Lavendar lived in Arkansas and died in his 70s. Lavendar and Melvin remained close friends until Ray's death.

"I met Melvin late in 1951 when the Air Force sent our newly-formed special weapons squadron to England," said Scholtens, who now lives in Tennessee. "Mel and I were second lieutenants, he a supply officer and I an electronics specialist."

When the men were told there was not enough on-base housing for officers, about 30 of them set off by taxi and train in groups of two or three in the late November darkness "to find shelter in a strange land," Scholtens said. He ended up with Melvin because of a mutual acquaintance.

"We were very lucky," Scholtens said. "We found refuge with Mrs. Lillian Todd, an aristocratic Englishwoman who had married and divorced an American. She owned a large house and lived there with her grown son Harry, in a cold but comfortable home."

The house was wonderful, as Scholtens remembered. "It was luxurious with four large rooms on the ground floor and five bedrooms for boarders on the second and third levels," he said. "Mel and I shared a room on the third floor under the eaves.

"There was no central heat. Only the kitchen was snug. It was warmed by a range and that's where we spent a lot of time having tea or whiskey. Wartime rationing still continued in England in 1951 and, perhaps to be comradely, whiskey was rationed on the base. But at 12 bottles a month, it was no hardship and helped keep many of us warm."

The Todds had a Jack Russell Terrier, Louis, who also liked a drink from the coal shovel. The house had a large drawing room off a central hall and big comfortable chairs by the fireplace. There was a gramophone in the parlor. And all the boarders had breakfast together before driving to the base.

It was 20 miles to the base and the Americans bought little English cars to drive back and forth each day. Melvin was the first to buy a car — a Ford Consul — and "was as generous in transporting his friends as he is in every other way," Scholtens said. "Melvin is not one who keeps to himself. He shares his time, his knowledge, and his belongings with everyone."

Until the wives of the married officers arrived, the Americans played a lot of poker, Scholtens remembered. "Melvin introduced us to Druthers," he said. "Melvin is superb at poker, especially Druthers. Perhaps that is linked to his generosity."

Early on, Melvin took to going into London on weekends, as did many of the others. A problem they discovered was finding gasoline, as most of the gas stations were not open on Sunday. "Mel had to be very careful to fill up on Saturday in order to get us home, sometimes through pea-soup fog, on Sunday," Scholtens said. "We may have contributed something for the rides he gave us, but not much. Of course cheap gas was available on the base, so there was no great hardship."

When the men arrived in England, they were told that any single officer stood a 90 percent chance of marrying an English girl.

"That proved true for both Mel and me," Scholtens said. He had met a girl working at the base who lived with her family in a flint cottage in the woods.

Melvin, left, served as best man at the wedding of Bob and Maureen Scholtens. Also pictured are Bob's new father- and sister-in-law.

"It reminded me of an Aesop fable," Scholtens said. "There was no electricity or running water, but lots of togetherness." Mrs. Todd gave Scholtens and his fiancée Maureen a huge engagement party, inviting everyone they knew, serving champagne from antique glasses etched with stars. Nearly 60 years later, Scholtens said his daughters have the surviving glasses.

The couple married in Harborne, a suburb of Birmingham, in the church where the bride's parents had been married. Melvin and Jasmine were there and Melvin served as best man.

"Mel went back to the states after a year and a half and I went back after two years," Scholtens said. "Jasmine and my wife were good friends and we stayed in touch over the years."

Melvin and Gary Long on the Thames River. During his years in the Air Force, Melvin spent most of his time in England.

In 1989, Melvin organized a reunion of the surviving 8th AFDS officers and they have met annually ever since. They have come to Shangri-La on Grand Lake in Oklahoma and, in 2007, the reunion was held at the Skirvin Hilton hotel in Oklahoma City.

"Mel paid the bill for all 14 of us," Scholtens said. "His excuse was that the price of gas was so high he owed it to us."

Scholtens kept in touch with Mrs. Todd until she died in 1989. Harry died in 1984, just a month after Scholtens' last visit. After Scholtens' wife passed away, he remarried. His wife, Joan, also was part of Royal Air Force Lakenheath in 1951, and a friend of Maureen's.

During Melvin's forays into London, he usually stayed at the American Officers' Club. The club, known as Winfield House, had been donated to the American government. The three-story mansion had once belonged to Barbara Hutton; it was appointed with marble, tapestries, crystal chandeliers, polished wood, and elegant furnishings. The officers paid $1 a night.

"They put two officers in most of the rooms," Melvin said. "I was there often enough so the clerk, who was English, knew me by name. One weekend I checked in and the clerk said, 'Lieutenant Moran, this weekend I am putting you with Lieutenant Jones.' So I went up to the room, unloaded my suitcase, and as I was hanging my uniform in the closet, it became obvious that Lt. Jones had already checked in. It was also obvious that Lt. Jones was a WAC."

Melvin immediately repacked his suitcase and went downstairs. He told the clerk that he would have to have another room because Lt. Jones was a member of the Women's Army Corps (WAC).

"And the clerk said, 'I will never understand you Americans. We give you a wonderful room for $1 with a woman in it and you still complain!'" Melvin remembered.

Melvin loved England and loved being in the Air Force.

"Because I lived in an English boarding house, I had more opportunities than most to get to know the English people and they were wonderful to us," he said.

In college he had learned to play table tennis and became the base champion. He also joined a table tennis club in the city of Newmarket and played in leagues and tournaments around the country.

Melvin, with his table tennis team in 1952, became a champion table tennis player while in England.

During his stay in England, Melvin made the first of his seven visits to Israel. In 1952, only four years after Israel became a state, a chaplain-sponsored tour was announced and Melvin asked to go. "I was the only person on the tour who was not a military chaplain and I was also the only Jewish person," Melvin said.

A trip to Israel was not a vacation for Melvin, nor for most Christians or Jews.

"For virtually every Jewish person, there is a spiritual connection to Israel," Melvin said. "But for my family, it is more than that. For me, it is an immensely gratifying and amazing experience."

His first visit, however, left him thinking that Israel was simply one large desert.

"The ten-day tour was to cover Israel and some of the adjoining Arab countries," Melvin said. "Because there was concern that if officials in the other countries discovered that I was Jewish, I might not be permitted to leave, I remained in Israel for the entire trip."

The other two officers at Melvin's boarding house took the train to London several weekends in a row and returned with stories of a great guy — Peter Miles. He was a former United States Air Force officer, graduate of University of California at Los Angeles (UCLA), now working with the Central Intelligence Agency (CIA). Miles knew London very well, including theater and restaurant owners and many showgirls. He had an apartment with extra beds and invited the two officers to spend the weekend while he introduced them to London.

"My friends encouraged me to come to London with them to meet Peter, which I did," Melvin said. "Peter introduced me to a showgirl, a dancer-actress. She was a beautiful woman of Scandinavian descent. Her name was Lillemor Knutsen and we dated for several weeks. A few years later, she was selected Miss England. When Princess Grace of Monaco was married, Lillemor danced at her wedding."

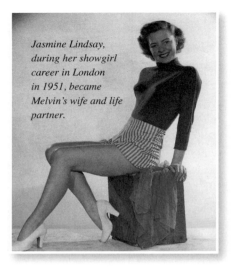
Jasmine Lindsay, during her showgirl career in London in 1951, became Melvin's wife and life partner.

Melvin's story is that Knutsen wanted to "dump" him. "She was kind enough to do it gently," he said. "She had attended dramatic school with another girl in the theatre by the name of Jasmine Lindsay. So Lillemor encouraged me to call Jasmine and ask her for a blind date. And I did."

One day Melvin's squadron commander called him into his office and asked him to tell him everything Melvin knew about Peter Miles. Melvin told him all he knew.

"He then told me that none of that was true," Melvin said. "Peter Miles had never gone to UCLA, had never been in the U.S. Air Force, was not in the CIA and not even an American. He was a British person posing as an American. He befriended Americans and then stole their cars.

"I am not certain to this day why he did not take my car, because he did have ample opportunity," Melvin said. "But he did introduce me to Lillemor and Lillemor got me the blind date with Jasmine. So it would be accurate to say that I met Jasmine as a result of my encounter with a car thief."

Melvin later married Jasmine and Knutsen married a Scotsman, Bill MacDonald. The four have remained close friends, visiting in England and Oklahoma many times since.

CHAPTER FIVE

Library Dedication

"The dedication of this institute, which will preserve and make a living reality of the dream of Ben-Gurion, is a momentous occasion in the annals of the state."
— President Yitzhak Navon

The Meyer Moran library wing was constructed as an extension of Ben-Gurion University near the kibbutz where Ben-Gurion lived his simple life. That morning in 1981, leaving Melvin feverish in his Jerusalem hotel room, the rest of his family was driven to the dedication by Joseph Jacobson.

Before Israel's creation in May, 1948 by a vote of the United Nations, Joseph Jacobson, David Ben-Gurion, and five others had been responsible for governing Israel in an underground council. Ben-Gurion served as the first prime minister and Jacobson, his closest friend and confidant, served in several other governmental roles.

Melvin had met Jacobson on a visit to Tulsa in 1980 and they remained good friends for the rest of the Israeli's life. He had been to Seminole to visit the Morans and each time the Morans came to Israel, Jacobson met their plane, waving them through customs like dignitaries. As a founder of the country, Jacobson was admired and respected throughout Israel.

Jacobson loved Jasmine's singing and especially her rendition of "Jerusalem of Gold." Melvin always joked that Jacobson put up with him so he could hear Jasmine sing.

On this day, Jacobson drove the Americans to the dedication. "Where is Melvin?" he asked as soon as they got into his car.

"He is ill," said Jasmine.

"Well, he must be very ill to miss such an important event," said Jacobson, concerned, as they drove away.

It took several hours to drive to Sde Boker, the site of the library. The car wended its way through the streets of Jerusalem, Israel's capital and largest city. The city is located on a plateau in the Judean Mountains between the Mediterranean and the Dead Sea. Modern Jerusalem has grown up outside the old walled city, which is one of the oldest cities in the world.

Jerusalem has been destroyed twice, besieged 23 times, and attacked 52 times. Its name is believed to include the Hebrew words for "legacy" and "peace."

Jerusalem is surrounded by valleys and dry river beds and, during Biblical times, was surrounded by forests of almond, olive, and pine trees. After centuries of warfare, neglect, and drought, it is now mainly buildings of Jerusalem stone and terraces built by farmers to keep the soil in place. Air pollution is caused by the large volume of traffic and emissions from factories on the Mediterranean coast 37 miles away.

Jacobson and the Moran family passed museums, theaters, civic buildings, and offices. There is little heavy industry in Jerusalem, where the economy mainly centers on religious tourism.

Upon their arrival at Sde Boker, the dedication began with a graveside ceremony at David Ben-Gurion's kibbutz, in recognition of the eighth anniversary of his death. Speakers included

Israeli President Yitzhak Navon, Deputy Prime Minister David Levy, and Education Minister Zevulum Hammer.

Dignitaries read selections of David Ben-Gurion's works and portions of the Talmud. At the conclusion of the ceremony, a dozen wreaths were placed on his grave.

"Year after year we renew our admiration for his wisdom, for his greatness," said Levy. "His contribution to the Jewish people lives on. Until his last day, he was tireless in his efforts on behalf of our people."

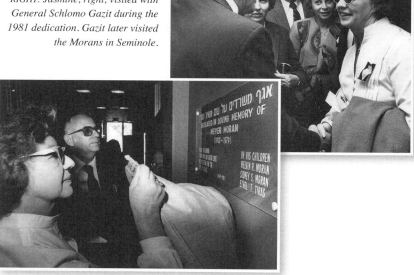

RIGHT: Jasmine, right, visited with General Schlomo Gazit during the 1981 dedication. Gazit later visited the Morans in Seminole.

Jasmine and her brother-in-law, Sidney Moran, unveil a plaque dedicating a library wing to her father-in-law, Meyer Moran, during a 1981 dedication in Sde Boker, Israel.

The president recalled how, on a trip to Negev, David Ben-Gurion first came across the settlers of Sde Boker and felt an immediate kinship of spirit with them.

"The dedication of this institute, which will preserve and make a living reality of the dream of Ben-Gurion, is a momentous occasion in the annals of the state," President Navon said.

The wing to the new library was beautiful and Jasmine sat in the audience next to Melvin's empty chair. She listened to the dignitaries and, at the appropriate time, took Melvin's place at the speakers' podium. She explained that only the gravest of illnesses would keep Melvin away from this dedication. Then she gave his speech as flawlessly and beautifully as the consummate performer she is.

After the ceremony, Jasmine sought out a telephone to call and check on her husband. She called the hotel room and there was no answer. She phoned back and had him paged, but again there was no response. She phoned a third time and spoke to the desk clerk.

"I'm trying to find my husband," she said. "He was very sick when I left him and now he's not anywhere to be found."

"Well, I don't want to scare you," the clerk said, "but about 10:00 a.m. an ambulance came and took a man away. That must have been him."

Terrified, Jasmine asked what hospital he had been taken to, but the clerk had no idea. She immediately went back to the university officials hosting the celebration.

"I was hysterical," she remembered years later. "We were supposed to stay through dinner, but I told them, 'I'm so sorry, but I have to get a car to take us back to Jerusalem. My husband has been taken to the hospital and I don't even know where he is.'

"They offered us a helicopter, but I said a car would be fine. They drove us back at breakneck speed."

The ride seemed to take hours longer than it had in the morning. As the Israeli desert streamed by her car window, Jasmine worried about her husband. Many women, not knowing if their husbands were alive or dead, would have dissolved into hysterical tears, but Jasmine Moran was strong. Her life had not been an easy one. Growing up in war-torn England, Jasmine's strength was developed at a very early age.

Jasmine Lindsay was born in Horn Church, Essex, England.

She was born in Horn Church, Essex. Her father worked as a waiter on a train. He was away a lot and, when Jasmine was four, he developed pneumonia and died. Jasmine herself caught pneumonia and was in the hospital for several weeks. During that time she developed scabies and had her hands tied to the bed so she would not scratch the sores.

Her mother, Lilian Davina MacPhee Burchell, had five daughters; one died at birth and another at three months. She raised the other three as a single mother, working days at a "knick-knack shop" and nights at a bus station. She had been a champion Highland dancer and a beautiful soprano. Sometimes she entertained at the aerodrome nearby.

"Our town was on a direct route between the ocean and London and we had an aerodrome a half mile away, which

used to be a training facility," Jasmine said years later recalling her childhood. "For 18 months, we were bombed 18 or 20
times a day. We had to hurry to get to school between bomb-
ings. They'd fire on anything below, including children. You'd
hear the bullets all around you; the sound was like a 'splat.'

"When the bombs came, the people went running in
every direction, usually trying to get home. It was pandemoni-
um," she said. "We children didn't have any sense. If we were
near the fire department, the firemen would run out and try to
capture a child under each arm and bring them inside to the
safety of the basement there. They'd almost throw you down
and run to get more children. You didn't always know who had
grabbed you and the noise would be deafening. The child under his other arm would be screaming, too. All I remember was
being airborne and screaming."

Jasmine grew up dyslexic, another hardship which forced
her to be strong at an early age.

"I never understood why the numbers and letters would
move around," she said. "I taught myself to read by focusing on
all the big words and averting my eyes to figure out the words
in between. I thought I was brain dead. It sure makes for poor
self-esteem."

Years later, as an older adult, Jasmine said something
"magical" happened. "I had terrible cataracts and when the
doctor took them both off, I was able to see things I hadn't seen
before," she said. "I was no longer dyslexic. The doctor said my
lenses had probably been malformed at birth."

At school, her teacher learned that Jasmine had a voice for
singing. "The teacher probably thought my loud voice could

cover the sound of the bombs," Jasmine said. "She probably thought, let's find her something she can do. She helped me decide my career."

At 10, Jasmine auditioned and was accepted at the Italia Conti school, where Anthony Newly and other English stars began their training.

"But we were as poor as church mice," Jasmine said. "My mother spoke to them and they said I could pay it out by working. I had my first West End show at 11."

West End in London is comparable to Broadway in New York.

After an hour-long train ride into London every day, Jasmine attended regular classes in the morning and private theatrical classes in the afternoon: elocution, Shakespeare, tap, ballet, and deportment.

After two and a half years, she began another school, Ada Foster.

"You don't graduate from theatrical school," she said. "Most of the time, at 15, a student would leave and go on to the educational part of schooling, like high school. I didn't go back to high school because I had a chance at 14 and a half to travel with the cast of 'Me and My Girl.' I lied about my age and said I was 15. After that, I always forgot the year of my birth."

Twice Jasmine played the now non-existent role of the maid Liza in Peter Pan. At age 12, she was hoisted into the air to fly with the children. She was strapped into a big leather harness, boned with metal, and hung from a thin wire.

At 14, Jasmine already was taking lessons in acting.

In 1951, when she and Melvin met, Jasmine was a successful actress.

"J.M. Barrie [playwright of Peter Pan] said the play could only be done at La Scala, which no longer exists," Jasmine said.

Even in the 1940s when Jasmine did Peter Pan at La Scala, the area was dangerous, especially for a child. She was escorted to the theater every day.

When she met Melvin, who was serving in the United States Air Force in London, she was 17 and performing in "Excitement." The two dated for 18 months until his tour of duty was over and he returned to the United States.

While in "Excitement" she auditioned for a role in the new show "South Pacific." It had opened five months earlier and two of the women already had left the show. For those two parts, 200 women auditioned. After several call-backs, Jasmine was given one of the parts, which she played for 18 months.

"Jasmine will tell you that her claim to fame is that she had a larger role in the show than did Sean Connery," Melvin always joked.

The desert passing by Jasmine's car window gave way to the first signs of city life. She turned and glanced at her daughter. Marilyn was no doubt as fearful for her father as Jasmine was. They gave each other a smile and Jasmine patted her hand.

"He's going to be fine," she said, maintaining a strong appearance for her daughter's sake. But inside she kept going back to the last time she had seen Melvin, looking half dead in the hotel room that morning. She thought of Melvin as he was supposed to look, full of life and fun, always moving through life with energy and enthusiasm. And she remembered back to their early days together and the very first time she had seen him.

It was early spring in 1952. She was 17 and he was 21. "It was a blind date," Jasmine remembered. "We were supposed to meet at the theater and he was late. Once a 350-pound serviceman started up and I strolled away, thinking that was my blind date. When he went off, I thought, 'Okay that's not him.' I had decided to wait five more minutes when he finally showed up."

"Mel" was a "97-pound weakling," Jasmine likes to say, quoting an old television ad. "He was very skinny and his uniform didn't fit him well, it was far too large," she remembered. "His feet were enormous."

One of the first things she noticed was that he was soaking wet. Melvin had been boating on the Thames with some friends and seaweed got stuck in the rudder. They had to dive in to free the boat. This made him late and caused him to show up for his blind date drenched and miserable.

Melvin drove Jasmine to the Officers' Club where he was staying in London so he could change clothes before dinner. As they drove up in front of the club, Jasmine saw a man on a telephone through the windows and remembered her pledge to call her girlfriend to report on the blind date at her first chance. As Melvin went upstairs to change, she found her way to the room with the phones and talked animatedly with Carol, telling her all that had happened so far.

"I saw men coming out of the next room zipping their pants," Jasmine said. "When I finished my call and came out of the room, everyone in the lobby stopped and looked. I tried to maintain my dignity. There wasn't a movement in the room. I turned to see the word 'Gentlemen's' over the door I'd just come through."

Despite her embarrassment over going into the men's room, Jasmine was prepared to enjoy her date.

"We ordered steak," Melvin said when he told the story of their first date. "Jasmine said she had never seen one so big. She cut off a piece and took it home to her family."

"I came from war-torn England," Jasmine said. "We could have two ounces of meat per person per week and two eggs. You couldn't live on that if you didn't grow things in the garden. Everything was rationed. Even in the 1950s, every penny counted and trash bags were always re-used."

The blind date did not go well from the beginning and was uncomfortable most of the night.

"He didn't talk and I couldn't stop," Jasmine recalled. "He gave one-word answers. It turned out he was sick, probably caught something swimming in the Thames. He threw up everything he had eaten."

But Melvin asked her out again.

"I said yes – I have no idea why," Jasmine said. "I guess it was just ordained by God. Afterwards, I went to visit my mom, who was in the hospital at the time. She asked about my date and I said it was dreadful. I'd embarrassed myself by going into the men's room."

"She told her mom our blind date was awful, but I was impressed and awed by her," Melvin said. "The second date went better."

After dating for a few weeks, it was time to meet Jasmine's mother, but in true Melvin style, that event became as tense and funny as the comedy skit which had become Melvin Moran's life.

"For the first couple of months, I hadn't met her mother because she was in the hospital with a serious illness," Melvin said. "Finally when her mother was released from the hospital, I was looking forward to meeting her and I was hoping that I would make a good impression."

Jasmine told Melvin that her mum had been raised by an alcoholic grandmother and hated alcohol. "Of course that would not be a problem for me because I seldom drank," Melvin said.

The week before the meeting, one of the officers riding in Melvin's little car failed to cork a wine bottle properly and it spilled in the back seat.

"My car smelled like a winery," Melvin said. He had a week to get rid of the smell.

"It was winter but I would simply go back and forth from the boarding house each day with the windows down," Melvin said. "I felt certain that the cool draft would get rid of the smell.

"Well, it didn't. At the end of the week, the car still smelled like a winery and because of the draft, I had the worst stiff neck anyone could imagine. My head was literally lying on my shoulders. So that was the way I went to meet Jasmine's mother."

After Melvin went back to the base on Sunday evening, Jasmine asked her mom, "Well, Mum, what do you think?"

Her response was, "He seems okay. But didn't you notice that he's deformed?"

The two dated for more than a year.

"Our squadron did top secret work relating to atomic weapons," Melvin said. "Because of that, every officer in our squadron was cleared for top secret information. We were the only officers on the base with this high clearance. So when it was necessary to have top secret documents couriered around the country, one of our officers had to be assigned to personally deliver it.

"I became friendly with the base officer who made these assignments. When he knew I was courting Jasmine, he frequently assigned me to deliver documents to London."

Melvin and Jasmine Moran, soon after meeting, walk along London streets.

Jasmine and Melvin's courtship included romantic outings on the Thames River.

Melvin's parents came to London to visit later that year and he took a leave of two weeks and vacationed with them in several European countries. "It was a glorious trip," Melvin recalled.

In Holland, they were told about a wonderful restaurant in Amsterdam called Five Flies. "We went there for an evening meal," Melvin said. "It was very crowded and we were told we could be seated immediately if we didn't mind being seated with another couple."

The three were seated with a middle-aged couple.

"From their appearance, it was my guess that they were from Yugoslavia or Czechoslovakia or someplace like that," Melvin said. "I asked the man if he spoke English and he said, 'a little.' For the next several minutes, we spoke to them very slowly and very phonetically. Finally I asked where they were from. He said New York. He thought we were the ones with difficulty in English."

The Morans saw Jasmine in "Excitement" and, when they met her, formed a good impression of her.

"I don't know if my parents knew I was getting very serious about the possibility of Jasmine becoming my wife," Melvin said. "My parents were very religious and I knew that it was very important to them that I marry someone of the Jewish faith. The religion of Jasmine's family was the Church of England, equivalent of the Episcopalian church. But it would be fair to say that she was brought up with very little religious upbringing."

"We hadn't attended church much," Jasmine said. "When I was growing up, they were afraid that if a bomb hit a church full of people it would devastate our town, so they divided up the services into five a day. My mother's assigned time didn't work for her because she worked all night at the bus station and days at the knickknack shop. And on Sundays, she often had to go to London on buying trips for the shop."

Always the entertainers, Melvin and Jasmine clown around during a London picnic outing in 1952.

It was shortly before Melvin returned to the United States that he proposed; they were in his car and he had no ring to give her.

Melvin's experience with women had been formed by his female relatives, the many girls he had dated, and the two crushes he had endured, one in high school and one in college.

"When I met Jasmine, I learned the difference between a crush and real love," he said.

"I was dating several people and hadn't realized he was that serious," Jasmine said. "I had to think it over. I had a friend, Stan, I always rode the train with. He thought we had a relationship; I thought we just went to parties with the rest of the cast.

"I asked Melvin if he couldn't stay in England. He said there was nothing there for him.

"The moment when I knew I would marry him was at a party with a lot of girls. We were joking around and somebody made a joke about Judaism. I said, 'Excuse me, I'm Jewish.' Everyone got very quiet and then everyone apologized. Later that night, my friend said, 'Jaz, you're not. Why did you say that? You really know how to break up a party.'

"I told Melvin the story the next weekend and he asked if I was thinking about taking on Judaism. Mel was more religious than I and I thought it would make him happy, so I started taking classes."

Melvin left England in June, 1953, and Jasmine followed that October.

"When I left, she thought she'd probably never see me again," Melvin said.

"I had no idea that Mel was relatively well off," Jasmine said. "Customs wanted to know who was sponsoring me. This was 55 years ago, before we had illegal aliens. His dad had to state on the forms about his finances and it was then that I realized they were a well-to-do family."

Jasmine spent the months before she left England fulfilling her contract in "South Pacific"; when the show closed in London, she was able to get out of her contract to tour with the cast. She left the wedding up to the Americans.

Jasmine began studying for her conversion to Judaism in early 1953. Melvin's chaplain, Rabbi Arthur Herzberg, arranged for her studies, which were taught by Rabbi Isaac Kaska. Her actual conversion took place after her arrival in New York.

"The rabbi who would be marrying us was our family rabbi, Rabbi Arthur Kahn, in Tulsa," Melvin said. "His brother was a rabbi in New York City and he converted Jasmine soon after she arrived."

Jasmine's mother was not so happy to see her daughter immigrate to the United States.

"She booked me on a cabin with another lady on the SS *Italia*," Jasmine said. "I had brought everything I owned and came alone to a place I'd never been before.

"It was awful. There was a hurricane, and a seven- or eight-day trip turned into 10. I was seasick from the second day. There were terrific winds. It looked just like the *Poseidon*, tipping from side to side. You could almost see the bottom of the boat. I lost nine pounds in 10 days.

"There was supposed to be one lady in my cabin, but there were three and they were all seasick — the smell was awful. I hung out on the deck where I could get to a restroom. Even the captain was seasick. I was so glad to see New York."

At customs, the agent asked Jasmine if she had anything to declare. "I said, 'only my wedding dress,'" she said. "He asked me if it had ever been worn and was nodding his head. I was so naïve. I couldn't believe anyone would ask such a question. Of course it had never been worn. Then he said, 'I need you to tell me it has been worn or I will have to charge you 100 percent in taxes.'

"Everyone here was so sweet."

Melvin met Jasmine in New York. He bought a Pontiac and together they drove to Tulsa.

"It was terribly hot," Jasmine remembered.

Melvin and Jasmine were married in the B'nai Emmunah Synagogue in Tulsa on November 22, 1953. Her dress, a size three, made of French lace by her mother's friend, a seamstress, had a collar that stood up, buttons below and "a lovely train."

"Melvin stepped on it in the first dance and tore it," Jasmine said. "It was so destroyed, I didn't keep it."

For the wedding, 250 were invited; 500 came. "So many thought their invitations had been lost in the mail," Jasmine said. "The extra folks were people who knew my father-in-law from the early years mostly. They loved him. There was not a crumb of cake left. It was a sit-down meal at the country club and they kept putting up tables. They managed to feed everyone."

Melvin and Jasmine with their wedding cake at their Tulsa nuptials in 1953.

The bridal couple with Melvin's parents and Jasmine's mother, the sole member of her family to cross the Atlantic for the wedding.

Jasmine's mother came for the wedding.
"I was a very fortunate girl," Jasmine said.
"My father-in-law was salt of the earth, a wonderful man.
My mother-in-law planned the wedding. They couldn't know if
I was marrying Mel for his money or what."

Mr. and Mrs. Michael Geselle
request the honour of your presence
at the marriage of their daughter
Ruth Jasmine Lindsay
to
Mr. Melvin Robert Moran
Sunday, the twenty-second of November
at six o'clock
B'Nai Emunah Synagogue
Tulsa, Oklahoma
Reception
at half after seven
Meadowbrook Country Club

*Two hundred fifty guests were invited
to Melvin and Jasmine's wedding.
Five hundred attended.*

*Newlyweds Melvin and Jasmine
Moran gaze lovingly at each other
soon after their 1953 wedding.*

Jasmine, who had grown up as the daughter of a single
mother, didn't know anything about how wealthy people lived.
In school, she had a friend, Marlene, whom she had visited and
was surprised to see how well they had lived.

"We all wore uniforms so I didn't know that she was well-to-do," Jasmine said. "She asked me to come home with her for a weekend. Mom talked to her mother and she said it was okay. Her house was magnificent. She had a butler, cook, maids, chauffeur. The house was furnished in antiques and her mother was so glamorous. The whole weekend was like that."

Later when Jasmine's mother asked when Marlene would come to their house, Jasmine said, "She can't come here. I can't let her see that we have to do everything ourselves.

"My mother was outraged. She said, 'You snooty little bitch. You will not behave like that.' Three or four weeks later Marlene came for the weekend. I was dreading it. There was nothing wrong with our house, but it wasn't like hers. When she came, we had to peel potatoes and carry out garbage. We climbed trees and did other things she'd never done before; she'd never been to the grocery store!

"I was 12 and it was a good lesson for me. You can have lumps of money in your pocket, and not know anything about the world."

By the same token, Jasmine, who had experienced much of life at an early age, was like a fish out of water in the United States.

They spent their wedding night at the Skirvin Hotel in Oklahoma City. While checking in at the hotel registration desk, Melvin signed simply, "Melvin Moran." When Jasmine asked him if he'd forgotten anyone, he was halfway to the elevator. He returned and added, "and Mrs."

Their honeymoon included the Grand Canyon and Las Vegas, Nevada.

That first morning in Las Vegas, Melvin got up early and went downstairs. He left a note joking that he had gone to win money for breakfast.

"I thought I'd married a Chicago gambler, like in the 1920 movies, a Mugsie Moran," Jasmine said. She locked him out of the room and packed to fly home to her mother. Only Melvin's pleading stopped her.

They continued their honeymoon in California, where friends took them to Reno for four glorious days. But their return to Oklahoma brought the newlyweds to begin their new life, and not in the metropolis of Tulsa. Within a few months, they found themselves in the small 1950s oil town of Seminole.

CHAPTER SIX

A Life of Service

"I wanted Seminole to be a good community in which my family and I could live and work."
— Melvin Moran

As soon as Jasmine and Marilyn closed the hotel door behind them that morning, Melvin tried to sleep. The heat pouring off his body did not seem to stop with the injection from the doctor and Melvin kept moving to find a cool place in the sheets. When the white cotton was soaked, it was time to move again.

Once Melvin tried to get up, but he could not. A terrible weakness had taken hold of him and he was unable to lift his head. He knew he was very sick, but was unable to do anything about it. What else could he do anyway? The doctor already had done what he could. Jasmine was gone to the dedication — she could not be any help to him. Maybe he should call the desk and ask for help. He was so thirsty, but a trip to the bathroom for water seemed as impossible as a hike across the Sahara Desert.

Melvin knew he did not have the strength to reach for the receiver. Even the thought of extending his arm toward the telephone caused his heart to pound like a jackhammer. Feeling weaker than he had ever felt in his life, Melvin lay in his sweat-soaked bed and knew the truth. He was going to die.

Most people, faced with imminent death, review the life they have lived. If Melvin had, he would have thought of his parents and all their sacrifices. He would think of his wife and children and all they had meant to him. He could think of his career and of his life in volunteerism and community service. That thought would have taken him back to the period just after he returned from the Air Force, just after he and Jasmine moved to Seminole. It was a very meaningful time of his life. Although his parents had always encouraged him to give back to the community, the early part of his marriage really set the stage for Melvin's life of community service.

The year was 1954. He had moved his pregnant wife to Seminole, a small town in the throes of an oil boom.

"Seminole was full of bootlegging, drinking, and prostitution," Jasmine said. "Seminole then seemed like the movie 'Chicago.' It was dangerous."

Melvin's dream of comedy writing had faded when he learned the beginning salary for comics. Besides, his degree in business had prepared him to join the family business.

"My father was in Tulsa and his business was in Seminole," Melvin said. "He wanted a family member there."

Meyer Moran was 60 now and the brother-in-law he had left in charge was in his 50s. It was time to think of the next generation. Meyer sent Melvin to Seminole to learn the business from the bottom up. He started as a roustabout, then moved up three years later to be his uncle's assistant.

"I worked long hours, from 7:00 a.m. to well after dark, six or seven days a week," Melvin said. "But it was the best thing I could ever have done. The knowledge helped me to do the job 100 times better."

Even working long, hard hours, Melvin's sense of humor could not be tamed.

Once when replacing the pump at the bottom of a well, the pump got stuck and the crew had to pull the tubing with the rods, a procedure known in oil country lingo as "stripping the well."

"I remember a stripping job on one of our leases in Yeager, the Martha Long," Melvin said. "I called my office and asked that Jasmine be called and told I would be late for dinner because I was 'stripping Martha Long.' When she got that message, she wondered what kind of business I was really in!"

Melvin was making $400 a month with room, board, and health insurance when he was discharged as a first lieutenant from the United States Air Force. This new job paid $300 — and from this he had to house and feed his wife and begin his family. They bought the house at 717 McKinley for $11,000.

Jasmine had become pregnant right away and she was sick and miserable. She cried herself to sleep every night because of the stifling heat and the backbreaking household tasks long before most people had dishwashers and microwave ovens. She tried hard to adapt to life as a married woman, but the homesickness was devastating.

"When I first saw Seminole, I thought it was the bowels of the earth," Jasmine always said. "It was dangerous. If not for our nice neighbors, I would have gone home. Charles and Wanda Sims were sweet and kind. They banded together to make me feel welcome."

Melvin took his bride to Oklahoma City or Tulsa on the

A LIFE OF SERVICE

weekends to the theater or other cultural events, trying to help
her assimilate. "I tried to make things as much like home for
her as possible," Melvin said. "The first year was very difficult;
by summer the temperatures were 110 and 112. She had a
terrible time with the weather and also the food. It took a long
time for her to get used to tea bags."

Things did not get better when, about two years after they
arrived in their new hometown, Melvin was called to serve on
a grand jury.

"While Melvin was sequestered, there were calls at night
saying something bad was going to happen to us," Jasmine
said. "I was terrified most of the time. Our neighbors said
they'd sleep with their windows open and if anything happened
to scream like hell. Our neighbor was a big man, six feet four,
and he said he'd come over."

"I didn't know it, but there was a lot of corruption going
on in our county, then," Melvin said. "At this time, the alcohol
prohibition law was in effect in Oklahoma. Yet alcohol was
almost everywhere. There were all sorts of payoffs connected
with illegal alcohol. And there was significant other corruption
as well. But I was naïve and didn't know any of this."

In 1956 or 1957, a petition was circulated and a grand
jury was called to investigate the corruption. Only 24 names
were drawn for the jury pool.

"The 24 of us met in the chambers of Judge Bob Howell,
a very fine and respected judge from Holdenville, who was assigned this duty," Melvin said.

The judge ruled that everyone over 65 could be excused.
People who were sick were excused. People who had small

children at home were excused.

"When everyone who could legally be excused was, there were only 10 of us left," Melvin said. "Judge Howell talked two of those who had been excused into serving. So it wasn't a question of getting the best 12 out of the 24. It was a question of taking whoever was left."

Seminole banker Ed Roesler was selected jury foreman and Melvin was selected clerk.

"Those 12 persons were among the most dedicated people I have ever met," Melvin said. "They were determined to do good and clean up the county."

They were in session for more than a month, listening to 100-plus witnesses. At the end they indicted the county attorney and the man who had served just before him and recommended the disbarment of five local attorneys.

They cleared County Judge David Cook, who had been charged with wrongdoing. Cook had tried to clean up the corruption so the guilty framed him: one evening Cook received a call from a woman saying she was in desperate trouble and needed to see him. He agreed to meet her late that evening in front of the post office. The county attorney agreed to let a Sasakwa inmate accused of manslaughter go free on condition that he drive his pickup into Cook's car at the post office. At the same time, the inmate was to leave liquor inside the judge's car. The county attorney was on the spot at the time of the "accident" and arrested Cook for drunk driving. The county attorney then offered to drop charges if Cook cooperated with his schemes.

After the grand jury exonerated Cook, he later became a

respected district judge in Oklahoma City.

Melvin and Roesler met with representatives of the Oklahoma Bar Association regarding their recommendations for disbarment of the five attorneys. The Bar Association representatives told them there was already a file of wrongdoings on the attorneys and that the information they brought would make the file thicker.

"Prior to our indictments, and directly because of the actions of certain attorneys, insurance in Seminole and Creek counties was higher than anywhere in Oklahoma," Melvin said.

But as to the indictments: one of the members of the grand jury was a card-carrying honorary deputy sheriff so the indictments were quashed.

"That man had no more authority than anyone, regarding law enforcement," Melvin said. "But the attorneys argued that having this card made him a sheriff and a sheriff cannot serve on a grand jury." The first judge ruled that the juror was not a sheriff, then he recused himself. A second judge was appointed and made the same ruling, then he recused himself. A third judge was appointed and he ruled that the juror was a sheriff and therefore the indictments were quashed.

"While this was a disappointment to the jurors, the bad guys all left town," Melvin said. "Seminole from that day forward became a much, much better community and I am proud that I served on that jury."

As a result of his service, Melvin learned that his community was not the nice, quiet clean place he had believed. "It was obvious to me that if good people do not become active in their community, then bad things are going to happen," he said.

"I was living and working in Seminole and I wanted Seminole to be a good community in which my family and I could live and work."

In 1961, Melvin filed for an open seat on the Seminole City Council. As a Democrat, he had two Democratic opponents. He won in the primary and then was successful in the general election against a Republican opponent. He served seven two-year terms, never again drawing an opponent.

For the rest of his life, Melvin credited the grand jury for causing him to see the need for public service. He led his city as councilor and mayor for 18 years, serving on the Chamber of Commerce, local civic organizations, and state boards from bi-partisan think tanks to educational, tourism, and economic capacities. He spoke wherever he could, encouraging people to become involved, and was successful in getting Seminole citizens to run for office, and in encouraging good ethical candidates at the state and even federal level.

"It is difficult to convince people to run for councilman," Melvin said. "There are frequently controversial issues and people become unhappy when you vote against the way they think you should vote.

"So why do councilmen, once they are elected, run for re-election again and again? Easy answer: When you are part of an entity that has accomplishments, there is immense satisfaction. And I truly believe the satisfaction of serving and seeing accomplishments, for which you had some part, is the reason for long service by many council persons."

The connection between Melvin Moran's public service and his lifelong dedication to his religion has been pointed out by his longtime friend, Robert Henry, who in later life nominated Melvin for the Oklahoma Hall of Fame.

"Melvin taught me about tzedakah," Henry said. "It's often translated as charity, but it's really righteousness, which encompasses justice, too. The essential point of it is that righteousness is its own reward. You do good not to get something for it but because the prophets tell you to do good.

"There are different levels of giving in tzedakah, levels of charity, with the highest being an anonymous donor to an anonymous donee, with no one other than God and you knowing that you're trying to do right. You see that in Melvin's life. He is the most dedicated person. Melvin knows how to run a business and he can almost do it on automatic pilot," Henry said. "He does that in a half day and the rest of his day and night are spent on every good cause."

CHAPTER SEVEN

A Man of Faith

"I think we have a responsibility to be good citizens because we are representing our religion."
— Melvin Moran

His experience with the grand jury and his lifelong dedication to community service were only a few of the things Melvin might have contemplated that morning in Jerusalem. With the fever raging, his body becoming weaker, and his heart threatening to burst from his chest, Melvin was thinking of meeting his maker.

He always had been a religious person, starting from his childhood. His parents had been staunchly Jewish and had encouraged their children to follow their religion. They had gone to temple, ate kosher, and observed the Sabbath. Melvin had followed in their footsteps, but it had become harder and sometimes impossible, while serving in the military or working six or seven days a week on a well-servicing unit.

The Moran family, including aunts and uncles, were the mainstays of the Jewish congregation in the Seminole area. At one time there were 40 families attending Seminole's Hebrew Center. For 50 or 60 years, there had been Sunday school in Seminole's temple, but Melvin could see their numbers beginning to decrease.

"I keep my Jewish faith alive because I truly believe in it," Melvin thought. "I believe in the traditions and the history. I think we have a responsibility to be good citizens because we are representing our religion. That's what I've tried to do."

Melvin always believed that Jews were supposed to help repair the world: help people, no matter where they are or what they are doing. About a half dozen people a week sought Melvin out in his office in Seminole to ask for help — people having an operation or families without money needing assistance to pay their electric bill. And then there were the regular charities and fundraisers.

Whatever the request, Melvin's policy was to never turn anyone away. Jasmine had once told him that some of those people probably went straight to the liquor store with the money he gave them and urged him to be more selective. The next time someone came in with a cause that did not seem very important, Melvin told them he could not give them money.

"I felt so guilty that a few days later when someone came in for the same cause, I gave them all the money I could and I just could have hugged them for coming back and giving me another chance," Melvin recalled.

"I think that charity is just something we're taught and we try to do. If it's a disaster, the Red Cross, the Salvation Army or anywhere around the world, I think that we should all try to help in whatever respect we can.

"My father was extremely charitable and I hope I've been able to follow that example."

One of the tenets of the Jewish religion is tikkun olam; it teaches that Jews should make the world a better place and that, when they die, the only thing left is their memory and the deeds they have done. With death staring Melvin in the eye, he hoped he had done all he should have.

CHAPTER EIGHT

Family Tales

"I remember the routine when I was a boy of Dad coming home from work, the dog running down the hall and jumping into his arms with me right behind him."

— David Moran

Jerusalem's heavy traffic slowed the car bringing the Moran family back to Melvin. While they had traveled at high speed over the miles of highways between the Ben-Gurion University and Jerusalem, now they were moving at a snail's pace. At times they stopped entirely; traffic lights that should have stopped them for only a minute kept them stalled for 10 minutes as traffic from the other direction filled the intersection.

Marilyn watched her mother from the corner of her eye. She could see Jasmine's strength, although she could also see her physically reigning in her panic. She had watched her mother for years and knew her very well. An outgoing and emotive woman, she was doing her best to keep the British "stiff upper lip."

Marilyn tried to focus on the traffic outside. She willed it to move, and when it did not she practiced deep breathing — anything to keep from screaming. She tried drawing on the inner strength her parents had imbued her with, trying to bring forth the patience she had seen in her father all her life.

She could hardly stand to think of how he had looked when she left him. She could not believe it was the same man who, just last night had told jokes and laughed at himself when the joke was on him. His dry wit had been a mainstay of her childhood and her life until now. To see him so sick was scary.

She had been her parents' firstborn, arriving in September, 1954, at Seminole Municipal Hospital. Marilyn had heard the story a million times. Like most of Melvin's stories, he made her birth hilarious.

"On television and in movies, I had seen where the mother didn't reach the hospital and the baby was born en route," Melvin said. "And in most of those cases, the father helped with the delivery in a car or taxi. I always had a fear of that. We lived three blocks from the hospital; I thought that was an awfully long way."

When Jasmine had her first labor pains, Melvin rushed her to the hospital. The staff said it was not time yet, so the Morans went home. A few hours later, Jasmine had additional labor pains, so Melvin rushed her to the hospital again. Again they were told it was too soon and were sent home. The third time, Melvin rushed her to the hospital again.

"Poor Jasmine was pretty well worn out by then," Melvin said. "And the hospital personnel said, 'just leave her.' Twenty-four hours later Marilyn was born. I thought it was a very close call."

As were most fathers of that generation, Melvin was at home in bed when he was called and told about his new baby.

"They thought I wouldn't carry her to term," Jasmine remembered. "I was as sick as a dog. I kept losing weight. If I'd smell anything, I'd start vomiting. All I wanted was walnuts in the shell. I ate them like a squirrel. Mel was all over the county looking for them."

By Jasmine's due date, Melvin "was a basket case," she said. There were 27 hours of hard labor before tiny Marilyn arrived.

"Back then they gave you hardly anything more than aspirin," Jasmine said. "They didn't want to slow the labor. I chewed the bar of the bed, but there was no relief. Marilyn only weighed five pounds six ounces. I had weighed 12 pounds myself. But she was beautiful. White as a sheet and colicky, but beautiful."

Firstborn Marilyn Moran arrived at Seminole Municipal Hospital in September, 1954.

Melvin and Jasmine after the birth of their first child.

Melvin cuddles with Marilyn in 1956.

New "mum" Jasmine shows off firstborn Marilyn.

Marilyn was sick all the time. She could not take breast milk nor cow's milk. The couple went to a man they knew who raised goats, where they bought milk and boiled it, then ran it through cheesecloth. At last the baby was able to keep something down.

According to her mother, Marilyn was always the one who "caught things" and had problems with her health.

"We all caught the measles and chickenpox together," Jasmine said. "Dr. Davis came over to check on the children and told me, 'I guess you haven't looked in the mirror.'"

Melvin, who never confessed to any culinary abilities, was pressed into service during this period.

"Jasmine was very ill; the least I could do was bring her breakfast in bed," he said. "So I made the only thing I knew how to make – a peanut butter sandwich. And she ate it. That day for lunch, I served her another peanut butter sandwich. She got out of bed and made supper."

Since then he has learned a little bit about cooking; he can now make a good cup of tea.

"Once while Jasmine was in Canada visiting her mother, I fixed my own supper," Melvin would tell their friends. "I called her that night and was very proud of my accomplishment. I made myself fried chicken, peas, and mashed potatoes. The fact that this was a TV dinner did not diminish the pride in my accomplishment at all."

Melvin always told everyone that neither he nor Jasmine knew a great deal about parenting when their daughter arrived. When Marilyn was a few months old, she was ill and they felt certain she had a fever. Melvin knew there was such a thing as a baby thermometer, but he had never seen one. He bought one at Stanfield Drug Store and brought it home.

"Neither Jasmine nor I could figure out what one was supposed to do with it," Melvin said. "I called Cecil Stanfield, the drugstore owner, and asked him if he could explain to me what one does with a baby thermometer. Mr. Stanfield was somewhat embarrassed to discuss it and he simply told me to read the instructions."

Melvin explained that he had read the instructions but still could not figure them out, so Stanfield asked him to bring it back and he would show him.

"When I handed Mr. Stanfield the thermometer box with

the thermometer in it, he became even more embarrassed," Melvin said. "What he had given me was a box for a baby thermometer all right, but what was in the box was not a baby thermometer. It was a glass tool used for the artificial insemination of horses. We have no idea how that instrument ended up in that box. It was a glass tube, similar to a thermometer. It had numbers on it that had no relationship to temperature. And it had a small stainless steel ring on it; I have no idea what that was used for."

Elisa was born in April, 1957, almost three years after Marilyn. David was not born until 1963.

The Morans with daughters Elisa and Marilyn in 1957.

"They were wonderful children," Melvin always said. "During their formative years, I frequently worked seven days a week and often 10 or more hours a day. I was unable to spend as much time with my children when they were young as I should have. Jasmine has been a wonderful mother and deserves the lion's share of credit for the goodness in our children."

For Elisa's birth, Jasmine went to Tulsa, where Melvin's gentle mother, Elsie, lay dying of liver cancer at the age of 54. "Far too young," Melvin said.

Daughters Marilyn and Elisa in 1960.

The Moran family grew to include son, David, in 1963.

The Moran children, ca. 1966, grew up surrounded by love and laughter.

"We hoped she'd see the baby before she died, but she died two or three weeks before, a very painful death," Melvin said. "Elisa wasn't born when she was supposed to be."

The Morans moved from 717 McKinley when Elisa was little, buying a house at 1910 Phelps, where they lived for the next 17 years.

When son David was born, Melvin and Jasmine were expecting a third daughter.

"When the nurse came out and told me we had a son, I asked her to go back and make sure," Melvin laughed.

When Melvin was at home, they shared in diapering and even feeding the babies. "One night, I put the bottle in a pan on the stove, then fell back to sleep," Melvin said. "We were awakened to a terrible explosion and milk on the ceiling."

On the type of father Melvin was, David would say, "I remember the routine when I was a boy of Dad coming home from work, the dog running down the hall and jumping into his arms with me right behind him."

It was at this time that Melvin realized that Jasmine had finally assimilated into Seminole's culture. "She still used her English expressions, but one day in 1965, I felt she had finally adjusted to Oklahoma," Melvin said. "That evening she came home and said, 'Mel, I am just plumb tired.'"

Like Melvin, she has come to love Seminole so much she has said she cannot imagine living anywhere else.

"If I fainted on the street in almost any city in America, I fear that I might lay there for days without anyone noticing," Jasmine said. "If I fainted in Seminole, I would be picked up before I hit the ground."

The children's stories about growing up Moran are just as funny as Melvin's.

"My Dad was an interesting man," Elisa said. "He was active in politics and business, but he truly wanted to be a comedy writer for TV. To that end, he spent much of our childhood giving us comedy sketches as part of our lives.

"Like when he leaped onto a moving merry-go-round. He did this with grace and ease. Unfortunately, he miscalculated the direction he should leap. He was last seen rolling around on the floor of the carousel, between the horses and the legs of the startled parents already on the thing! We pretended we didn't know him."

That would also be true of his appearance at Elisa's class in high school. Melvin was mayor at the time and, with all the dignity his office could muster, he came to speak about government. He gave quite an impressive lecture which he topped off by sitting down hard on the floor when the chair rolled out from under him.

One of the more "infamous" incidents in their family history was when Marilyn and Elisa were playing tag behind their house and the house of their neighbor, Les Jones. There was a wooden fence behind the Moran house and a barbed wire fence behind the Jones house.

It was a hot summer evening and the girls were wearing shorts and tank tops. It was getting to be dusk and hard to see. Elisa chased Marilyn, who ran "smack dab" into the barbed wire fence and became fully entangled.

"After extrication, it was clear that Marilyn was covered, head to toe, in cuts," Elisa said. "Dad's remedy was to put a separate band-aid on each tiny cut. This left Marilyn, barely able to walk, because she was covered in about 100 Band-Aids.

"Days later, when we had pulled off all the Band-Aids, along with all her arm and leg hairs, she was left with only a few scars!"

Melvin had other, more successful health remedies, too.

"I have vivid recollections of having aching legs with growing pains at night," Elisa said. "Dad would come in with two baby aspirins. No, he didn't give them to me like you would think any parent would —he would carefully place one on each knee and pronounce that I was cured! I never thought it was too funny, although Dad found it very amusing each of the 400 times he did this!"

Soon after Marilyn started school, the family took a trip to

Disneyland in California, any child's dream.

"I loved every part of it — well, except for the Huckleberry Finn boat ride," Elisa said. "That one still leaves me in fear. I can't see a jar of huckleberry jam, even today, without a sinking feeling!"

It was summer and very hot. There were long, snaking lines for every ride. The family stood for what felt like hours in every line for every ride. While in a long line for the Huckleberry Finn boat ride, Elisa said she started day-dreaming. The line inched forward and when they were near the front, she reached up for her daddy's hand and took it.

"I looked up to say something to him, and to my chagrin, I found I was holding hands with some man I'd never seen before!" Elisa said. "I started screaming and crying. He was quite startled to find himself holding hands with a strange child who was screaming her head off."

She looked desperately around for a familiar face and found none; every member of her family had boarded the boat without her. The happy ending came when, as the boat was pulling away from the dock, Melvin jumped off and came back for her.

"The less happy ending is that Mom, Marilyn, and my Aunt Davina took the boat ride, then returned to shore," Elisa said. "But after standing in that line for hours and being scared out of my wits, I didn't ever get to even take the ride!"

Elisa always said Marilyn comes out looking pretty good in the family stories.

"After all, she is sweet, kind, mature, looking out for her siblings, and just standing innocently by while I get hurt and maimed," Elisa said.

But one summer day when family friends Steve and Cindy Underwood came over, Marilyn and Steve decided they'd had enough of Cindy and Elisa.

"They were bent, not just on revenge for things we'd done," Elisa swears. "They were bent on actually murdering us."

They lured the younger girls into the tornado shelter, a small round cement room underground in the back yard. It was reached by lifting a heavy door and going down about 10 to 12 steps into a dark, dank, smelly space full of spiders and bugs. There was one air space in the ceiling.

"There was always an inch or so of water in the bottom of the cellar that never dried out," Elisa said. "All in all, a most dismal place to spend time, much less to die!

"After some subterfuge or another, they got us to go into the cellar. As we descended the steps, they slammed the heavy door shut on us and locked us in! It was dark and full of spiders! We were yelling to get out, when we heard an ominous noise… it was the garden hose being inserted into the air vent, then being turned on full blast!"

The girls jumped onto the bench seats to avoid the rising water. There was four or five inches of water in the cellar when Melvin came out to check on the sound of running water.

"He discovered the deed and rescued us from our watery tomb," Elisa said. "Even with the evidence right in his hand [the water hose he had pulled from the air vent], my Dad was convinced it was just a silly little joke and that no real harm was intended. The culprits escaped from their escapades without punishment of any kind!"

Elisa's sense of humor, obviously inherited from her comedy writer wannabe father and her entertainer mother, can make any family story hilarious.

She tells of the time she got in the biggest trouble of her life. She and Cindy took matches from Cindy's house into the creek bed behind the houses. Because it was August, it was very dry outside. They made a ring of rocks and were pretending to be cowboys lighting a camp fire. For awhile, they lit the matches and threw them into the rocks and sand, where they sputtered out.

"Then, Janis Chappell came over and suggested throwing it in the grass," Elisa said. "Cindy said 'yeah,' lit a match, and threw it. Whoooosh!! The grass went up immediately and within a split second, the dry, Oklahoma summer grass was ablaze. It spread out of control! Cindy tried to stomp it out and burned the soles off her shoes. I leaped our fence and ran home and got Dad, who was babysitting that day."

Melvin ran out and the other neighbors ran out and started beating the fire with wet blankets but it was too far gone. All they could do was try to keep it from reaching any of the many houses that ringed the golf course. The fire department sent three trucks and after a valiant battle, put the fire out.

"No houses or fences got burned which was quite a miracle," Elisa said. "The firemen yelled at us, our parents yelled at us, and we were all banned from playing together for about a month.

"Worse, everywhere we went, everyone in town knew we were the kids that ruined the golf course for the entire season. People in Seminole took their golfing very seriously so we were quite the pariahs until, mercifully, the grass grew back in again."

Years later, David and his friend set the golf course on fire again with the rocket they built for a school project. Jasmine tried for 90 minutes to extinguish the fire with wet gunny sacks.

"Again, the Seminole Fire Department came to the rescue to put out the Seminole Golf Course after yet another one of the Moran children had set it ablaze," Elisa said. "Again, we were pariahs until the grass grew back. But, we have the distinction of being the only family in Seminole, dare I say all of Oklahoma, even all of the United States, where two children both burned down their local golf course. I ponder the question as to whether our arson tendencies had any effect upon Dad's decision not to continue being the mayor of Seminole."

Other important lessons that the Moran children learned from their parents included this: When a child is leaning over the toilet in the middle of the night, making retching sounds, no matter how much compassion you may feel, you must never, ever, ever, reach down and swoop that child up.

"I was the child in this story," Elisa said. "And Dad was the hapless, and ultimately very sorry, parent. I clearly remember trying to throw up, then being swooped into the air, immediately throwing up down the back of Dad's pajama shirt, then being suddenly back down on my own two feet again."

Even when their children were little, Jasmine and Melvin were animal lovers and developed into animal rights' activists early on. One funny story involves the gift of a parakeet named Humphrey.

"Humphrey was a very smart little bird," Elisa recalled.

"He could open his cage by himself. He would get out and fly around the house, alighting on the tops of the curtain rods."

Their vivid memories include Melvin sneaking up to the parakeet with a dish towel, leaping energetically and throwing the dish towel at Humphrey, the concept being that he would capture the bird by getting him under the dish towel.

"Where in the world he came up with this method is one of those mysteries lost in our past," Elisa said. "Anyway, there is Dad, sneaking up on the bird. There is the bird, sitting on the curtain rod, appearing to be interested in other things. There is Dad, getting the towel into prime flinging position. There is the bird, still looking in another direction. There is Dad, taking aim. There is the bird, still not at all interested. There is Dad throwing the towel. There is Humphrey, cleverly lifting off and darting away from the towel with room to spare."

Despite hundreds, maybe thousands, of attempts, Elisa does not remember a single incident of Humphrey being caught by the sneak, aim, and fling method of dish towel capture.

Then there was the tiny kitten abandoned in the yard at the pipe company. She would run through the pipes and get covered with oil, then come into Melvin's office and get under his desk. The kitty would climb up the back of the drawers and fall asleep in the desk on Melvin's papers, covering them in oil and tiny footprints.

"After a few days of this, we got to bring the kitty home," Elisa said. "Ming Ming lived with us for several years and we loved her very much. Dad was also pleased because his paper-work was 'waaayyy' less oily when the kitten was living at our house instead of the pipe yard."

When Marilyn was about seven, she got a stuffed cow for a present. The life-like brown cow even had an udder.

"My parents were really bored," Elisa said. "I think that is the explanation why parents ever really have children – so they can make fun of them and relieve boredom."

As the family discussed how cows give milk, one parent would distract the children and the other would run to the fridge for a glass of milk, and place it under the cow.

"Then, they said, 'Wow, look! The cow gave milk!'" Elisa said. "We were really blown away! We thought that was cool. We tasted it and thought it tasted just like regular milk – it was even cold."

When they wanted to see it again, their parents complied! "We were easily distracted, read 'really stupid,'" Elisa said as another glass of milk appeared.

Maybe they should have left well enough alone, but then they decided because it was a brown cow, maybe it could give chocolate milk. When the glass of chocolate milk appeared shortly thereafter, Elisa said the kids were on to them! "We weren't too slow, were we?" she said, laughing.

When Elisa was six she liked to play with a girl named Dawn Chesser, who lived about a block and a half away. One hot summer day, Dawn came over and the girls were arguing about where to have a tea party. Elisa wanted to do it by the swing set where all proper tea parties should be. But, Dawn was insisting they had to have it in the creek bed behind the Moran house.

"You know how it is," Elisa said. "The tea party location is everything!

"One thing led to another and Dawn slapped me across the face! I couldn't believe it! I grabbed at her, and somehow the entire front of her shirt ripped off! I was standing there with a handprint on my face and she's standing there wearing sleeves, a collar and the back of her blouse! That's how Dad found us when he wandered outside."

Using all the skill he had learned from Dr. Spock, and a lifetime as a peacemaker, Melvin told the girls to shake hands and apologize.

"After shaking hands and apologizing, I went in the house," Elisa said. "I'm still feeling pretty darn good about the only physical fight [outside of siblings] I ever had. Remember, this took place at my house, so I just went inside. Dawn lived one and a half blocks away and had to walk home without a blouse! I think the winner here is pretty clear!"

Then there was "David with the broken neck."

When David was about five and Elisa was about 11, the family went to a carnival. There were little kid rides and being 11 Elisa believed she was too mature to ride them. But David wanted to go on the little kid roller coaster.

"He wanted it bad. Really bad," Elisa said. "The problem was he was afraid to go by himself. Dad was too big to fit into the seat so I got roped into going against my will."

The ride consisted of a train of cars that went in a circle on a track and went up and down some mild hills, maybe thrilling for David, but at 11, Elisa was mortified.

"After one or two circles, David leaned over and told me he was going to puke!" Elisa said. "Talk about an ungrateful kid! Here I publicly humiliate myself by riding this thing and then he is going to throw up on me to boot! What could I do? I did the only logical thing — point his face in the opposite direction of mine and hold his head that way until the end of the ride."

But Melvin, on the ground watching, saw it very differently. "In some fashion he managed to convince himself that David had broken his neck and that I was protecting his delicate vertebrae," Elisa said.

"Keep in mind, this is the kiddie ride, going maybe one mile an hour, barely going up or down any hills. How Dad concluded David's neck got broken is quite beyond me."

Elisa said Melvin began running and yelling at the ride operator to stop the ride because his son was injured, making quite a scene when the ride finally rolled to a gentle stop.

"He ran over and grabbed David's neck to immobilize his head and was thanking me for saving him," Elisa said. "We had to tell him that I was simply trying to avoid being hit by splatter when David blew.

"Now, you'd think he'd be relieved to hear his son wasn't permanently paralyzed. I guess, deep down, he was. But, he couldn't hide the disappointment that his heroics in getting the train stopped had really been for nothing."

The children's memories include fun times with Jasmine's mother and her second husband, Michael Geselle.

"Grandpa was my partner on the Moran Family Vacation from Hell," Elisa said. "For some reason, the adults in our family seemed to think that putting eight of us in a station wagon and driving through the blazing hot desert to California would be fun."

Elisa, in her inimitable comic style, painted the scene with Mom and Dad in the front seat with Marilyn between them and Grandma, David, and Cousin Bruce in the middle seat.

"Now, pan back to the rear of the station wagon, keep panning, back, back, no, further back, almost there – you know – that miserable seat in the very back, the one with absolutely no air conditioning and no air," she said. "The one in which the occupants must ride backwards? That's the one. This is where I sat with Grandpa, day in and day out, traveling backwards all the way to California.

"Now, also remember Grandpa was huge, so he took up three-fourths of the seat and four-fifths of the little air that was getting to the back, and now you'll have an idea of my version of the trip to California."

An hour into the trip, the car was literally hit by lightning, burning a mark across the top of the luggage rack and shaking up the occupants of the car. Shortly thereafter, they had a flat.

"Then, to top off the trip as one of the most miserable in our lives, coming home through Texas, Dad decides to save a penny a gallon on gas," Elisa said. "He lets a little old lady in a shower cap and bathrobe fill our tank.

"We made it four miles to the Oklahoma border when the entire car filled with foul fumes and the car died. We just rolled into a gas station when the eight of us exited that vehicle as fast as eight people can get out of a car. The gas attendants were cracking up and said they knew exactly what was wrong – the bad drip gas we'd bought across the border."

When Elisa was 14, the family took a trip to Colorado. At Mesa Verde, something went wrong with the car. If the engine was turned off, it would not start again.

"So, we saw Mesa Verde like this," Elisa said. "We'd drive to a viewing spot. Four people would get out and leave one person in the car with their foot on the gas peddle, revving the engine. The other four would run at top speed down the trail, quickly scan the ruins, read none of the informative information, race back to the car, and we'd move to another spot, where a different person had to stay in the car revving the engine.

"It was ridiculous and I couldn't tell you to this day, what we saw there. However, the one bright spot was that I was only 14 and thought it was pretty cool to get to sit in the driver's seat and press on the gas peddle with the engine running!"

Not long after, Melvin had the job of teaching Elisa to drive.

"Dad never loses his temper," Elisa said, a fact backed up by his co-workers, friends, and everyone else who knows him. "He is always very calm and cool. On my first driving lesson, I'm going along at about two miles an hour on a dirt road. About two miles ahead of us, a kid pulls out of a driveway on a bike. Dad, being overly cautious, says we should pull over and let him go by.

"Considering he is two miles away, I knew he wouldn't get to us for quite some time. I said I was fine and I could go a bit further. Dad calmly said that it would be better if we stopped.

"I said, 'You want me to stop now?'

"He said, 'Yeah, go ahead and stop now.'

"I said, 'Are you sure? I'm really fine.'

"He said, 'Yeah, let's stop now.'

"I said, 'Now?'

"He said, 'Yes, now.'

"I hit the brake, Dad hit the windshield hard with his face," Elisa said.

"He very calmly said that he thought that was enough for today. We got home and he had a giant goose egg on his forehead.

"But, he taught all three of us to drive with barely another scare or injury!"

The children — and many of his friends — joke about Melvin's driving.

"We've found that Dad has two undeniable habits while driving," Elisa said. "First, if Dad gets into telling a story, he takes his foot off the gas. The longer the story, the slower we get. There are times when we've been going down the highway doing a good clip of 75 mph when Dad starts telling a story. By the end of the story, we are inching along with every other car passing us!"

But this habit is much preferred over his other one. Melvin tends to be so interested in the storytelling going on in the car, that he frequently does not hold his foot on the pedal in a steady manner. Instead, he steps on the gas, lets up, steps on it, lets up, steps on it, lets up....and on and on. Meanwhile, he is rapt in the story and does not notice that the passengers are all becoming quite sick from the jerkiness of the car ride.

"We had all noticed this years ago but for some reason, none of us ever mentioned it," Elisa said. "It wasn't until about 10 years ago that we all admitted we felt sick when Dad got going on a story while driving the car!"

The kids tell funny stories about Melvin's love of ketchup. "He puts it on everything," Elisa said.

"I learned all about 'ketchup sandwiches' from Dad. Mom, on the other hand, thinks ketchup is an abomination and shouldn't be allowed anywhere near decent food."

Once Melvin had ordered Jasmine a present for their anniversary, but it had not come in time. He did not want her to be disappointed, so he got a box and wrapped it up beautifully. To give it weight, he filled it with rocks. He thought this would give her a gift to open and then when the real one arrived, he would give that to her.

"Mom had seen the box, hefted it, heard the movement inside and had been intrigued for several days before the big event," Elisa said. With great anticipation, she opened the box on her anniversary and found, to her great dismay, the box of rocks.

"She was not a happy camper," Elisa said. "However, she bided her time. The next day, Dad came home for lunch as usual. He sat at his place at the table. To the great amusement of Marilyn and me, Mom brought his plate to the table — a giant plate full of rocks covered with ketchup! Ah, revenge is sweet!"

Not all of the stories are funny; some are inspirational.

Elisa tells of her childhood in the early 1960s when many cities in the south were not integrated. Seminole, where the Moran children attended elementary and high school, was integrated when the school for blacks burned down and the town could not afford to build another.

"However the pool was 'white only,' as were public fountains, restrooms, many stores, and restaurants," Elisa remembered. "I have a really clear picture of the summer our pool became integrated.

"Things were happening everywhere, Martin Luther King was leading marches in the South and to Washington, peaceful black protestors were being attacked by dogs, and goons in police guise were spraying them with water hoses. Little girls were blown up in their church basement, and two young Jewish men were murdered with a young black man trying to get blacks registered to vote in the South.

"But, one summer in the late '60s the movement came to Seminole," Elisa said. "There were no police dogs, or water hoses, or marches. There weren't sit-ins, or riots. Instead, it happened at the swimming pool. The town declared it was open to everyone!"

The first day of that summer the whole Moran family was at the pool at opening time. It stands out in Elisa's memory because her mother had never been to the pool; she could not swim. But this day, she was there with the rest of them, first thing when the pool opened.

"As the black kids jumped into the pool that they'd never been allowed to swim in before, I remember sitting on the edge listening to two white biddies tsking that they'd never let their kids swim with those 'n......s,'" Elisa said.

"My parents, in full view of the rest of the town, told Marilyn and me to go get in. We were the first white kids in the pool with the black kids. Looking back, it's a small thing. But it sent an important and powerful message I've never forgotten."

The decision to open the town pool to blacks would have been made by the Seminole City Council, of which Elisa's father was a member throughout the 1960s. Asked if there was debate or controversy over desegregating the pool, Melvin said he did not remember. The position of a gentle Jewish peace-keeper on the City Council, however, may well have tempered the integration issue in Seminole, violently controversial in most other places across the nation at that time in history.

Marilyn smiled at the funny stories that had been part of her family's heritage for as long as she could remember, but then her mind traveled back to the reason for this trip as the car inched toward the Jerusalem hotel.

Although she could not know how close her father was to death at this moment, she thought of the old saying: be kind to strangers because you never know when you might be hosting an angel unaware.

"I believe Melvin Moran is an angel, unaware of the fact himself," she would later say about her father.

"He believes to the depth of his soul in the Jewish teaching to do a mitzvah — a good deed — every day. But a good deed for Melvin isn't a single daily act; it's a continuous way of life."

She knew what people thought when she said anything like this. It's natural for the daughter of a good man to look up to, even idolize him. But hers was not that kind of story.

"I had no idea exactly how amazing my father was until, as an adult, I began to reflect on my childhood and to really listen with adult ears to the appreciation of others," she said.

"The first time I was asked about my own passion for volunteerism, I thought, 'What an odd question! It's just what everybody does – no big deal.' But when asked a half dozen times, I came to realize that, while helping others was a natural part of Moran family life, it was not the norm in most house-holds."

As a child, Marilyn always remembered her father bringing home dirty, smelly, unkempt people who showed up at his office in search of a handout. It was not in Melvin's DNA to look the other way when someone was down on his luck. So he and Jasmine would feed them, give them a comfortable bed for the night, and money in their pocket to begin the next day.

"I remember wondering how these down-on-their-luck people all found their way to my father's office," Marilyn said. "After all, Seminole, Oklahoma, isn't exactly a major metropolitan magnet. Hobos apparently have a network and Melvin Moran's office was a famous way-station for people in need."

During the 1970s, the Moran family, including parents and grandparents, gathered for Marilyn's confirmation.

Melvin has the honor of giving away his daughter, Marilyn, at her wedding.

As she grew up, Marilyn once asked her father why he helped people who might be taking advantage of him.

"Dad smiled and used that teachable moment to pass on his belief about people," Marilyn said.

"I can't live my life being suspicious so I choose to believe that everyone is good – and almost everyone proves me right," Melvin told her.

The result was that Marilyn had never met a person who thought ill of her father. "Quite the contrary; total strangers learn that I am Melvin's daughter and begin telling me their favorite funny, and always kind, 'Melvin story,'" she said.

"This angel is happiest with hands-on projects. He sees a woman in tears at the bank because the teller says she is overdrawn. What does Melvin do? He spends hours and hours helping her balance her checkbook, create a monthly budget, and learn to live within her means."

Most people with means donate to organized charities and so does Melvin Moran.

"But he also gets his friends to help Mom and him actually cook the Christmas dinner for anyone who can't afford a nice meal," Marilyn said. "And he actually shops for every gift for some 100 children and 600 adults in my hometown who otherwise won't have a nice Christmas. After filling hundreds of shopping carts, he also personally delivers groceries for another very lucky handful of families.

"Thanksgiving and Christmas may be times when everyone feels more charitable. But for Melvin Moran those are just two days — he is looking for ways to do good deeds the other 363 days, year in and year out," Marilyn thought. "I don't believe he misses a single day."

Charity begins at home and Marilyn had seen it happen over and over: Melvin and Jasmine befriend strangers worldwide, making such an indelible impression that, once their fortunes improved, these strangers-now-friends make pilgrimages to Seminole from foreign countries to visit the "kindest Americans" who helped them when they needed it.

Despite his remarkable love of humanity, Melvin's humility would not allow him to be the center of attention.

"He really doesn't like the limelight and he sincerely believes that what he does isn't particularly remarkable," Marilyn realized.

There is a song that describes Heaven as a place where people will meet and are thanked by those they have helped, sometimes unaware of the difference they had made in others' lives.

"If that description is true, Heaven will need crowd control when Melvin Moran arrives," Marilyn thought, smiling.

CHAPTER NINE

Heaven's Gate

"I truly and sincerely believe that I died that morning."

— Melvin Moran

At the moment, Melvin was very close to making the trip Marilyn envisioned. The heat of the fever seemed no longer to matter; the terrible weakness was all he could feel. He could no longer move his legs or arms. The pounding of his heart seemed to be weakening. He slipped into unconsciousness.

There have been many documented incidents of people recalling their own deaths. Such reports can be found in the Bible, the Koran, and the Tibetan Book of the Dead, as well as in modern research.

Those who have died and come back tell of hovering over themselves, on operating tables or sickbeds. They see themselves and can later recall conversations or things that happened, all while doctors and nurses are trying to revive them. They are clinically dead — sometimes for hours —and all evidence proves that. But still they know what the doctors are doing, what the nurses are saying; they see their family members crying.

Most people who are able to later relate the episode, report eerily similar experiences: a bright light, sometimes a tunnel or vortex, figures in the light, who sometimes are deceased family members, sometimes a deity or spiritual presence. Sometimes there are strange sounds. The deceased person can feel anxiety or peace. Usually they feel no pain. They feel their body rising toward the light and know they are dead. Sometimes they see beautiful vistas or hear a voice. Sometimes they report the absolute dissolution of their body.

On this day in Jerusalem, Melvin Moran felt his spirit float away from his physical self.

"I saw myself in bed and dead from above," he said. "I must have been floating. There were no lights, no vistas, and no dark tunnel. The room was light enough for me to see myself in bed. There were no other sounds and I was pain free.

"I was anxious because I was not ready to leave this earth," Melvin continued.

"I didn't see G-d or anyone else."

But Melvin heard God's voice and answered him.

"I had a two-way conversation with Him, but I never saw Him," he said in relating the episode.

Asked if the conversation was in words or by telepathy, Melvin said he remembered words.

"Later that afternoon I tried to recall the sound of His voice, but I couldn't," Melvin said.

"I couldn't recall if He had a deep voice or a light voice. I don't recall Him speaking with an accent.

"When I remembered it later, I felt that my not being able to recall the sound of His voice was by design."

The conversation was brief — a couple of minutes or so.

"I told G-d that there were many things unfinished in my life and I asked to go back," Melvin said. "I did not elaborate, but I was referring to taking care of my family."

And, as the prayers of righteous men are heard and answered, Heaven was moved by Melvin's request.

"G-d asked me to do something and I promised that I would," Melvin said.

"I have thought about and recalled that promise hundreds of times. And that promise continues to direct what I try to do with my life."

Asked about the promise, Melvin is firm.

"I shall not divulge what that promise is about, but it is something that I am still attempting to do," he said.

When God left Melvin, he fell into a peaceful sleep and awakened several hours later.

"From the time that Jasmine and Marilyn left me until the time I woke up fever-free was about seven hours," Melvin said.

"I have no way of knowing if my conversation took place shortly after they left or if it took place just before I woke up."

But he vividly remembered every word of the conversation.

"I tried to remember the face, form or voice of G-d, but I couldn't," he said. "My mind suddenly had a blank slate."

However, he found himself miraculously well.

"I remember being very thirsty," Melvin said. "So I got dressed and went downstairs to the hotel restaurant and drank a large glass of orange juice."

In his life, Melvin only told the story of the Jerusalem incident three times — once, to his wife; the second time, to his friends Donna and Ivan Terry, when they traveled to Israel with the Morans several years later; and third, to Marci Donaho, a friend who was later instrumental in an important project in his life.

"When my children read this book, it will be the first time they will have heard this story," Melvin said.

"I truly and sincerely believe that I died that morning," Melvin continued. "Most people would say that, with a temperature of 107, I was having a hallucination. Skeptics will say I was asleep and it was a dream. The fact that I was in the Holy City of Jerusalem could have accounted for the 'dream' about G-d. That my temperature was back to normal could be explained by the fact that the Israeli doctor gave me some medication early that morning.

"If this explanation were true, it seems that after I had that very high temperature, I would have awakened in a weakened state. But I wasn't weak. I felt just fine," he said earnestly.

"I do not actually know what happened. But if I were to take a lie detector test, and if I were asked, 'Did you die that morning?' I would respond yes. And if I were asked if I had a two-way conversation with G-d, I would respond yes.

"And I would pass the lie detector test with flying colors."

CHAPTER TEN

Aftermath

"Melvin does not change; he's the same Melvin as in high school."

— Mervin Aptak

The car squealed to a halt in front of their hotel in Jerusalem and Jasmine, Marilyn, Sid and Ione, and Jeannie and Jerry jumped out and ran to the door of the hotel, each terrified about what they would find out about Melvin's condition.

As Jasmine reached for the handle of the plate glass door, it opened and there stood Melvin.

"He looked like a shiny new penny," she said, amazed even years later telling the story. "I couldn't believe it.

"I said, 'Melvin what are you doing?'

"He said, 'I woke up and felt so good, I went for a walk. Are you ready to go out to dinner?'

"He was lucky I didn't kill him right there."

Raymond Moody, author of *Life after Life*, found that most people who survive near death experiences usually have their lives altered. He says they generally become more altruistic, less materialistic, more loving. Other researchers found near death experience survivors see the good in all people. They sometimes act with naiveté and allow themselves to be taken advantage of. They often lose their taste for ego-boosting achievements.

It would have been hard for Melvin to become kinder, gentler, or more charitable.

"Even in high school, if Melvin thought anything bad about somebody, he'd be quiet or find something positive to say to counteract it," said his old high school friend Mervin Aptak. "Melvin does not change; he's the same Melvin as in high school."

"Mel is one of the most likable people in the world," agreed Maynard Ungerman, who knew Melvin from his teen-age years. "Nobody who knew him could dislike him, even as a kid. Even back then, Mel was like the perfect kid."

"Mel is a lot like our father, always helping people," said his sister, Jeannie Tiras. "Our father helped a lot of people and Mel took over for him when he passed away. I know Mel still takes care of the family members in Israel. He's always been that way, does it quietly, doesn't want a plaque.

"I'd love to tell even one mean thing Mel ever did, but there is nothing. Our brother, Sid, might pick on the little sister, but Mel never did. He always treats people fairly. If he owes you money, he pays the next day."

Jeannie said the only thing they have ever argued about is when she feels Melvin is "trusting to a fault." Jeannie said. "I'd rather have him that way, of course. Sometimes he makes excuses for people he shouldn't. There have been times when he should have opened his eyes about people, but he always sticks up for them.

"After Father died, if someone said someone else wasn't equipped to handle things, Mel would say, 'It was good enough for Daddy, so it should be good enough for us.'"

"Melvin Moran, as much as any person I know, represents the Jeffersonian ideal of civic republicanism," said Robert Henry, Melvin's close friend for many years. "He's a man of talent and success who devotes his time to his community — in this case a very large community encompassing city, state, nation and globe — in order to ennoble and empower that community to work for the common good."

"Melvin always puts himself last," said Kenneth Henderson, who credits Melvin for bringing him to Seminole, where he bought the historic Grisso Mansion. "He always makes sure the other person goes first. He's a rare person and, to me, he exemplifies the spirit of giving and doing. He leads by example and that's the best way to lead."

"I've known Melvin in all capacities since the 1970s," said his business associate Gene Rainbolt, chairman of BancFirst. "He has the greatest integrity of any person I've ever met. His loyalty is incredible, his enthusiasm is contagious. His commitment is persevering, his energy is unflagging. His curiosity and creativity are unequaled."

One would be hard pressed to compare Melvin's life before his death experience in Jerusalem with his life afterwards and find that he had become even more altruistic or more generous.

However, most people would say that, on that day in 1981, at the age of 51, Melvin's crowning achievement in life was still to come.

CHAPTER ELEVEN

A Friend to Israel

"Jasmine thought the country and its people were wonderful and was amazed at the progress... I think her positive attitude may have rubbed off on Congressman Edwards."

— Melvin Moran

Melvin finally did get to tour the Ben-Gurion Library, a one-on-one tour led by Joseph Jacobson. He also toured the modest kibbutz near Beersheba in the Negev, the Israeli desert in southern Israel, where David Ben-Gurion lived even while he was prime minister of Israel.

"It is as modest a home as a home can be," Melvin said. "There were only three or four rooms and most of them were filled with books from floor to ceiling. Ben-Gurion spoke seven languages. He learned these languages because he wanted to read books in the language in which they were written."

Ben-Gurion kept a diary, in which he wrote nearly every day of his life. "I was given access to the diary," Melvin said. "It was remarkably detailed. There was one entry where he said that he had just returned from a meeting and it was 10:00 p.m. Then he wrote about 10 pages giving details of the meeting.

"Another entry was written on the day he was married. He had extensive writings about what happened that morning. Then he wrote two words: 'married Paula.' And then he had extensive writings about other things with which he was occupied the rest of that afternoon and evening."

Because Melvin's father loved and appreciated Israel so much, he frequently donated to Israeli entities and especially to Ben-Gurion University, a practice Melvin continued. In November, 1983, a small building on the campus of the Ben-Gurion University was named in memory of Melvin's mother, Elsie Moran.

ABOVE: Melvin visited privately his father's memorial after the 1981 dedication.

Melvin visited with Joseph Jacobson, who became a close personal friend of the Morans until his death.

ABOVE: Melvin at the 1983 dedication of his mother's memorial at Ben-Gurion University.

Melvin and Jasmine cut the ribbon on his mother's memorial at the Ben-Gurion University in 1983.

"My brother, my sister, and I, along with our extended families, were all invited to the dedication of this building," Melvin said. "And we were all present. All three of our children came with us, along with Jasmine's mother, stepfather, and her sister Helen, who all flew in from Canada."

On that trip, they became acquainted with the president of Ben-Gurion University, General Shlomo Gazit.

"Like many Oklahomans, we said to 'come and visit us in Oklahoma,'" Melvin said. "We never imagined that he would come, but he did."

While visiting the Morans in Seminole, the general told them the real story of the "Raid on Entebbe."

"General Gazit had headed Israeli military intelligence for many years," Melvin said. "It was General Gazit who devised the rescue plan of the hostages at Entebbe."

On June 27, 1976, Air France Flight 139 from Tel Aviv to Athens was hijacked by two Palestinians from the Popular Front for the Liberation of Palestine — External Operations (PFLP-EO) and two Germans from the German Revolutionary Cells (RZ). They diverted the flight to Benghazi, Libya, where it stayed on

Melvin and Jasmine listened to guest speakers memorialize Elsie Moran during the 1983 dedication in Israel.

Melvin had interesting sites pointed out to him during a 1983 trip to Jerusalem.

the ground for seven hours for refueling. It then took off and set down at Entebbe Airport in Uganda.

At Entebbe, the four hijackers were joined by three additional terrorists supported by the pro-Palestinian forces of Uganda's President Idi Amin. They demanded the release of 40 Palestinians held in Israel and 13 other detainees imprisoned in Kenya, France, Switzerland, and West Germany. If their demands were not met, they threatened to begin killing the hostages on July 1.

The hijackers held the passengers hostage for a week in the airport's transit hall, during which time they were visited by Idi Amin himself. Some were released, but 105 of the 248 passengers and 12 crewmembers remained captive. The Jews were singled out to be killed first.

After a week, the hijackers announced that the airline crew and non-Jewish passengers would be released and placed on another Air France plane, brought to Uganda for that purpose.

Flight Captain Michel Bacos told the hijackers that all the passengers were his responsibility and that he would not leave them. The entire crew followed suit. A French nun also refused to leave, insisting that one of the remaining hostages take her place, but she was forced into the awaiting plane by Ugandan soldiers. A total of 83 Israeli and Jewish hostages remained, as well as another 20, which included the plane's crew.

On the July 1 deadline, the Israeli government offered to negotiate with the hijackers in order to extend the deadline to July 4. On July 3, the Israeli cabinet approved a rescue mission.

After days of collecting intelligence, four Israeli Air Force C-130 Hercules transport aircraft flew secretly into Entebbe Airport under cover of night, without aid of ground control. They were followed by two Boeing 707 jets. The first Boeing contained medical facilities and landed in Nairobi, Kenya. The commander of Operation Entebbe, General Yekutiel Adam, was aboard the second Boeing that circled Entebbe Airport during the raid.

Many documentaries and movies have been produced detailing how the raid was carried out. They all agree that it lasted less than 30 minutes and all seven hijackers were killed. Three of the hostages also were killed and10 were wounded. Forty-five Ugandan soldiers were killed; only one Israeli commando died during the operation.

"When the hostages were rescued and they, along with the French aircraft crew, were on the plane headed back to Israel, General Gazit ordered a diversion for that aircraft," Melvin said.

The plane had been headed for Ben-Gurion Airport, located between Jerusalem and Tel Aviv. The world's press was at the airport waiting to hear the stories from these hostages. But General Gazit ordered the plane to land at a nearby military base. He met the plane and ordered the passengers into a building where he addressed them.

"General Gazit told them that they would soon be reboarding the plane and taken to Ben-Gurion Airport where they would be questioned by reporters from around the world," Melvin continued the story that the general had told him. "He told these rescued hostages that he would like for them to fully talk about how they were hijacked, how they were treated, and what Idi Amin said to them when he addressed them.

"And finally, he asked them to tell the press that they were awakened in the middle of the night and suddenly herded on an aircraft and that was how they obtained their freedom. The general asked them not to describe what actually happened during the rescue because 'we might have to do this again someday.'

"The rescue had occurred several years prior to the general's visit to Oklahoma and he told us that there have been movies, television shows, and books written about the rescue, but, 'nobody got it right,'" Melvin said.

"The general said the hostages, including the French crew, were so appreciative for being rescued that they never told the whole story...which was the way the general wanted it."

Melvin invited the general to speak at the Hebrew Center in Seminole, and invited several of his non-Jewish friends to attend, as well.

"He called me once and said General Shlomo Gazit from the Entebbe incident was coming," said Robert Henry, the Morans' close friend.

"Would you like to have dinner with this guy? What an opportunity to talk to somebody who was a huge player in world history," Henry said.

"The general is a man of peace, which is so interesting. He is celebrated for this daring raid, but he was really sorry that it had come to that. He wanted to talk about peace and the United States being more careful in its foreign policies, to have more discussions and talk to people more before resorting to intervention."

Melvin has made a total of seven trips to Israel. When he went for the dedication of his mother's wing at the library, he called an Israeli journalist he had heard speak in Oklahoma City. She had invited him to visit her when he returned.

"She invited Jasmine and me and Jasmine's sister, Helen, to her home for dinner," Melvin said. "Her husband was a fascinating man; he'd been an Israeli ambassador to several countries and, in his younger days, he'd been an Israeli spy in Russia."

Another guest that night was Israeli Prime Minister Shimon Peres. He sat next to Melvin, who asked him if he had ever been to Oklahoma.

"His response was that of a diplomatic statesman," Melvin said. "He said, 'Of course, many times. Visiting America without visiting Oklahoma would be like visiting Israel without visiting Jerusalem.'

"I was very impressed!" Melvin said.

"I said to him, 'If you come back to Oklahoma, I would be delighted to give you a tour of our oilfields.'

"His response was, 'I would much prefer to see your agriculture.'"

Later the Morans had the opportunity to visit Israel with a VIP trip sponsored by the State of Israel. Oklahoma City Congressman Mickey Edwards and his wife were invited and Israel state officials hand-picked two couples to join him: the Morans and Bob and Joy Heiman of Oklahoma City. Although the couples were invited, each paid their own way; they met the congressman for the first time as they boarded the plane.

"I had never been on a VIP trip before," Melvin said. "While we were shown the historic and holy sites, we also met the country's leaders. Everywhere Congressman Edwards went, the rest of us went as well."

They visited Prime Minister Yitzhak Rabin in his office and visited Shimon Peres, who was foreign minister at the time.

They went to Israel's parliament and visited with the leaders of all the major parties. They visited military bases and with military intelligence officials.

"At that time, drones were new and I was fascinated with them," Melvin said.

A drone is a tiny, pilotless plane, not much larger than a kite, run by engines the size of that of a lawn mower. Drones patrolled the Israeli borders and were constantly taking photos and forwarding them to military headquarters.

"It was amazing," Melvin said.

They spent several hours with Russian Jewish dissident Natan Shransky in his apartment. Shransky had been imprisoned in Russia for many years. When he was finally released, he immigrated to Israel. He had been hosted at the White House and by world leaders before serving as a cabinet minister in Israel.

"He lived in a very modest apartment, which was on the fourth floor of a very modest apartment house," Melvin said. "There were no elevators so he would have to trudge up four flights of stairs each time he wanted to go to his apartment. There was almost no furniture in his apartment. He had some folding chairs that he put out for us when we visited. He was an interesting and amazing person."

Melvin remembered Congressman Edwards voicing some skepticism about Israel when they first met him.

"Jasmine thought the country and its people were wonderful and was amazed at the progress," Melvin said. "She was so upbeat and I think her positive attitude may have rubbed off on Congressman Edwards. When he came back to the U.S., he became one of Israel's strongest advocates in the entire Congress."

Making a Name for Himself

"I sat on the constitutional board that certifies revenue, the State Equalization Board, along with the governor and the state treasurer. It was only appropriate that, when we estimated the price of oil, we'd turn to Melvin Moran."

— Robert Henry

When Melvin and Jasmine moved to Seminole in 1953, they planned to stay for three years and go back to Tulsa. It never happened and it was a choice with which they both agreed.

"I didn't want to live in Tulsa any more," Jasmine said. "Every town has its good and bad points, but this is where we choose to live our lives."

After several years on the well servicing unit as a roustabout, Melvin moved into Moran Pipe and Supply's office. He assisted his uncle, manager George Kahn, as co-manager and at the same time assisted Moran Oil's production superintendent, Cecil Rice.

By the mid 1970s, Kahn retired and Melvin co-managed the supply company with George's son, Mike Kahn. About the same time, he became principal manager of the oil company.

In 1981, Melvin's family sold their interest in Moran Pipe and Supply and he became the full-time manager of Moran Oil Company and Moran-K Oil LLC. Moran Oil is now Moran Oil Enterprises, LLC, and today Melvin shares the responsibility for it with his son-in-law, Elisa's husband, Gary Kleiman. Additionally, Melvin's brother, Sidney, and Sidney's son, Everett, are actively involved.

Oklahoma is a major oil producer, ranking fifth in the United States in 2008 and second in the production of natural gas. There are approximately 90,000 oil wells in Oklahoma producing an average of two barrels of oil a day, down from the 1950s when the average was seven barrels per day.

"Since leaving the Air Force, I have been involved in the oil business, which is a very exciting vocation," Melvin said. "There have been a number of peaks and valleys regarding the price of oil since I became involved in this business. The deepest valley was in 1986."

In 1985, the average price of oil was $28 a barrel. The price collapsed in January, 1986. For some period of time, the price dropped below $10 a barrel. For the entire year of 1986, the average gross price — the price paid by the purchasing company — was $14. A portion of that price goes to royalty owners and another portion for taxes. When the price was $14, the working interest owners received approximately $10.50, according to Melvin.

A study in 1986 showed that the average cost of lifting a barrel of oil to the surface was $15, meaning that, for every barrel of oil produced, the owners of the well lost $4.50.

The major industry of Melvin's hometown was oil and oilfield supply and service company firms, including his own.

"There were well over 150 energy firms in Seminole at the time the price of oil collapsed," Melvin said. "Probably 90 percent of them went broke and out of business. Of those that remained, most were only a shell of their former selves, as employees were necessarily laid off."

Melvin was convinced that the price of oil would come back.

"Our company kept all of its wells running and did not lay off a single person," he said. "For that period of time we borrowed money to keep the company alive."

This collapse of oil prices caused a recession in Oklahoma; in Seminole it caused a depression. The period where money was lost on every barrel produced lasted about three years. Homes were for sale on virtually every residential block. It seemed that almost half of the downtown businesses were closed.

"I've observed Melvin in every capacity," said his business partner Gene Rainbolt. "We went through some difficult times in the '80s. The oil industry and some banks were collapsing. Melvin always stayed calm, made prudent decisions, took no excessive risks."

Melvin has become an expert in the field, lecturing and advising even presidents on the subject, but he is humble about his accomplishments, usually telling them as funny stories on himself.

When Bill Clinton was president, Melvin was invited to the White House three times. The first time about 30 people were invited for a discussion with the President on economics. The group also met with the Treasury Secretary Robert E. Rubin and other officials.

"I don't think for a moment they had any interest whatsoever in what I might think about economics," Melvin said. "At that time, I was chairman of 'Oklahomans for Boren' and David Boren was our United States Senator. I feel certain that they [at the White House] were hoping that the President might be able to influence me and that I might repeat some of that to Senator Boren. I didn't."

As he was packing for Washington, Jasmine asked him if he was taking a camera. He told her he did not think it would be appropriate.

"After all, this was for an economic discussion," he said. "Well, I was the only one there without a camera."

He was invited again to the White House in 1996 by First Lady Hillary Clinton to discuss her healthcare initiatives.

"This time, I was not going to be the only one without a camera," Melvin said. "This small group of about seven people was seated around a table and I was seated directly across the table from Mrs. Clinton. When there was a pause in the discussion, I took out my camera and pointed it toward Mrs. Clinton. She immediately stopped talking and posed. And I snapped her picture.

"Well, I attempted to take the picture, but the battery in the camera was completely dead. Oh well."

Melvin was invited a third time to the White House as President Clinton was about to unveil his energy policy.

"About 30 of us were invited," Melvin said. "I was one of two from Oklahoma. In addition to meeting with the President, I also had the opportunity to meet with Vice President [Al] Gore. It was a thrill for me to be there. But I was very disappointed in the energy policy which the President announced on that day."

During the previous 10 years, 450,000 jobs had been lost nationwide in the oil and gas industry. After reading the new energy policy, a 36-page statement, Melvin told the local newspaper that he did not find one thing that would significantly help Oklahoma's independent marginal well producers.

"I told [Secretary of Energy Hazel O'Leary] how desperate things were for independent oil producers," Melvin said. "And I told them the two things we needed most were import fees or a floor price, which are basically the same thing, and our second priority is tax incentives for marginal wells, both ideas which were being studied by the Department of Energy."

At that time, the price of oil was $13 a barrel.

Melvin told the Clinton administration that if prices did not improve significantly, tens of thousands more jobs would be lost, tens of thousands of wells would be plugged and abandoned and thousands of oil producers would be out of business.

"They can only produce at a loss for so long," he said.

Most of Melvin's predictions for the future of oil came true, said Robert Henry, who was serving in the early 1990s as Oklahoma's attorney general.

"I sat on the constitutional board that certifies revenue, the State Equalization Board, along with the governor and the state treasurer," Henry said.

The board has the responsibility of estimating revenues for the coming year, figures upon which state budgets are drawn.

"It was only appropriate that, when we estimated the price of oil, we'd turn to Melvin Moran," Henry said. Melvin has served on the board of the Oklahoma Independent Petroleum Association since 1980. He served as president in 1989. "We'd say, 'Hey, Melvin, send us a letter telling us what you think the price of oil will be' on any given day," Henry said. "He was an unofficial adviser to this board. I have retained one of those letters."

Melvin's letter to the State Board of Equalization states: "The price of oil has continued to be volatile…During the first week of January, I predicted an average posted price for Oklahoma Sweet during 1990 of $20 per barrel…Although the posted price at the moment is below that level, I feel very comfortable with that estimate and am bidding production with that assumption."

"For the first four months of 1990, the average price of Oklahoma Sweet was $19.94. He was six cents off!" Henry said. "Melvin is a person you can always turn to. But he'd never contemplate doing anything that would give him an economic advantage."

Melvin's business acumen and his perceptions are highly sought after. In the fall of 2008 he was interviewed by Ben Montgomery of Florida's *St. Petersburg Times* on the state of oil and gas in Oklahoma. His story was published September 22.

"My cousin, Suzy Morgan, lives near St. Petersburg, and she opened her newspaper that morning and was surprised to read a story about me on the front page," Melvin said. "She did remark that the story …aged me by nine years."

At noon the same day, Melvin had a phone call from someone purporting to be Melanie Marshall of BBC Television in London. She said she had read the *St. Petersburg Times* article and wanted a similar interview.

"I admit to being skeptical regarding the phone call,"

Melvin said. "I thought that it was highly unlikely that people in London would have seen the story from the Florida newspaper. And if they had, I felt that it was doubtful that they would want to spend the money to come all the way to Oklahoma to interview someone they knew nothing about. But I decided to wait and see if they actually would show up."

They set an appointment for 9:30 a.m. Monday, September 29. Melvin told his children about the call and the newspaper story that had aged him by nine years.

Always the comedienne, Melvin's daughter Elisa said that if BBC did come Melvin "should try hard to look wrinkled so they will not be disappointed."

Melvin spent hours on Friday cleaning his desk, although he still believed the call was a hoax. But on Sunday evening, Marshall called him, saying she'd just landed in Tulsa. She asked directions to Melvin's Seminole office.

"She also mentioned that she had not been certain that her plane in London was going to take off because it had been so foggy," Melvin said. "That remark made me doubly suspicious. London really does not have all that much fog, but it does have the reputation. And I thought perhaps she was saying that to make me think she really did fly in from London."

On Monday morning, Melvin's secretary brought in refreshments for the guests, "in case they should really come," Melvin said. Marshall said she would call when she was on the way.

"And I sat behind my clean desk awaiting their arrival," Melvin recalled. "There was no phone call and 9:30 came and went with no visitors. It was the same at 9:35 and 9:40 and 9:45. By this time, I felt certain that I had been had. It was a hoax and I had fallen for it hook, line, and sinker. However, at least I ended up with a clean desk."

But at 9:48 a.m. Marshall, who was a BBC producer, arrived in Melvin's office, along with Susan, who was an on-air interviewer, and Ian, the cameraman. Despite Melvin's surprise, the crew filmed for five hours in his office, around Seminole and on a nearby oil lease.

Melvin gave the BBC team his views on the global energy picture, along with the history of oil in Oklahoma, especially the Greater Seminole field. He showed them a working well and how it pumps the oil from the subsurface into the tanks.

"I told them that demand will likely equal supply within the next ten years so we need every alternate source of energy possible," Melvin said.

The interview was scheduled to be part of an energy documentary being done by BBC Television.

CHAPTER THIRTEEN

Hitting the Campaign Trail

"I wanted someone well organized, someone I could totally trust, someone who knew people, a civic leader. He was the ideal chair."

— David Boren

Adviser to governors and presidents was not the first way that Melvin served his community.

"Living in Seminole has shaped my life," Melvin said. "Seminole is an amazing city. And yes, I admit to having a decades-long love affair with this community. It is, I believe, a city unlike any other."

Because his experience on the grand jury in the 1950s showed Melvin that not all people were good, and that if the good people did not get involved, bad things happened, Melvin decided to get involved in community affairs and local politics.

"I campaigned for issues that were brought before our community for a vote, such as sales taxes, bonds, etcetera," Melvin said.

He was elected to the board of directors of the Seminole Chamber of Commerce and later to the Chamber presidency.

He had his first experience campaigning for a major office holder during the late 1950s and early 1960s, America's "McCarthy period."

"In my mind Senator [Joseph R.] McCarthy was a threat to civil liberties," Melvin said. "I remember picking up a *TIME* Magazine one day and reading a story

Melvin visited the Oklahoma State Capitol in the early 2000s.

about Oklahoma Senator Mike Monroney being the first senator to openly criticize Senator McCarthy. On that day, Senator Monroney became my hero."

In 1962, Monroney was running for re-election. Jim Monroe, a newspaper publisher in southern Oklahoma, called Melvin and asked him to serve as Monroney's Seminole County campaign chair.

"Because of my respect for Senator Monroney, I said 'yes' without hesitation," Melvin remembered.

Monroney carried Seminole County but lost the election to Henry Bellmon.

A long and warm relationship, one that went back to Melvin's return to Seminole in the 1950s, was strengthened when Seminole resident David Boren ran for state representative.

"I was so impressed with the representation he gave us that I immediately became an admirer and a friend," Melvin said. "I supported him for every election after that as he ran for re-election: representative, governor, U.S. senator. I was much honored when Senator Boren, in 1964, asked me to serve as chairman for Oklahomans for Boren."

"Melvin served as chair and treasurer of my statewide campaigns," Boren said. "I asked him because he was extremely well-known statewide, through the Oklahoma Independent Petroleum Association and the state chamber. I wanted someone well organized, someone I could totally trust, someone who knew people, a civic leader. He was the ideal chair. He had studied journalism and was very articulate. If the press called, the chairman of the campaign had to know the right answer; he was very talented in dealing with the media.

"Melvin made sure everyone got there and did what he asked them to do. He was good at organizing the meeting and, if people said they'd put up this many signs or bumper stickers, he'd check and make sure they did. It took a lot of time to carry out those responsibilities and he generously gave of his time."

Boren remembered a time when his campaign was going to a rural school event and ended up at the wrong rural school.

"But there was a crowd gathered for some other purpose and Melvin still got out and campaigned for me," Boren said. "It turned out wonderfully."

Melvin served as chair of the campaign committee for former District Judge Gordon Melson.

"I first met Melvin when I was living in Ada and ran for district attorney in 1966," Melson said. "He didn't get very involved in that race, but later on when I was appointed judge, he wrote me a very nice letter and helped whenever I had a contested election after that.

"We generally support the same candidates, although not always," Melson continued. "Melvin is a little more cautious than I am; I'm a little more outspoken. He tries to get along with everyone. If he has a fault, it's that he goes overboard trying to please everyone."

Melvin served as state or county chair for numerous other candidates running for local, state, or federal office.

"Without exception, these were folks who had no agenda except to help better our wonderful state," Melvin said. "And most of these folks, some of whom were elected and some of whom were not, became personal friends of Jasmine's and mine."

From 1961 to 1975 Melvin served on the Seminole City Council, first under Mayor Fred Adwan and later for Mayor Waldo Lilly. Melvin was Lilly's vice mayor for six years.

"Both Fred and Waldo were wonderful people and only

Melvin, second from right, was sworn in as a Seminole City Councilman in 1961. He served seven two-year terms.

desired to better their community," Melvin said. "And they did."

During this time, the publisher of the Seminole newspaper, Milt Phillips, became another of Melvin's heroes.

"What a terrific person," he said of Phillips. "He was so respected by our mayors and councilpersons that when we would go into executive session, we would invite Milt to join us. We knew he would not make public something that should not be made public. We kept no secrets from Milt and, when he gave us advice, we listened. He was, in my opinion, Seminole's number one civic leader."

From time to time people would encourage Melvin to run for mayor, but he always said he had no desire to be mayor.

However, Phillips asked Melvin to run for the seat left open when Mayor Lilly decided not to run again; Melvin could not turn him down.

"I respected him so much and had some idea of the sacrifices he had made to help our community," Melvin said. "So I agreed to run."

The two persons who financially helped Melvin's campaign the most were Milt Phillips and local oilman Jimmie Austin.

"Even though Milt was the one who had encouraged me to run and had contributed to my campaign, he did not editorially endorse me," Melvin said. "He did not endorse anyone. He felt that it was important that *The Seminole Producer* be there to work with whoever won the election. And I respected him for that."

Melvin's opponent was another city councilor, Bill Snell, a competitor in the oilfield equipment business and a good friend.

"Bill and I ran a very friendly campaign," Melvin said. "There was nothing negative from either of us. When we went out to do radio commercials, we traveled together."

Melvin knocked on every door in Seminole during his campaign, leaving business cards advertising the fact that he was running for mayor. When no one was home, Melvin would leave his card in their door to let them know that he had been there.

"On one particular day, I stopped at a house where no one was home," Melvin said. "I left my card in the door. I noticed that Bill had already been there, as his card was already on the door. On the back of his card, he had written, 'Sorry I missed you. Bill.'"

Melvin walked on another couple of blocks and began to think of Snell's handwritten note on his card.

"It was more personal than mine was," Melvin said. "So I walked two blocks back to that house, retrieved my card and wrote, 'Me, too. Melvin.'"

During his campaign Melvin committed one of the little faux pas that have made his life sometimes embarrassing, but always hilarious. He had read a front page story in *The Seminole Producer* about the death of oilman Frank Harber and commented to Jasmine what a fine person Frank Harber was.

"Jasmine said she never met him, but his wife was a lovely lady," Melvin said. He didn't know Mrs. Harber but Jasmine said, "You have seen her several times. She worked at the Vogue Style Shop. If you saw her again, you would recognize her."

About 10 days after Mr. Harber's death, Melvin was in Stanfield's Drug and heard one of the clerks refer to a woman in the pharmacy as Mrs. Harber.

"This woman did, indeed, look familiar and I thought that this was probably Frank Harber's widow," Melvin said.

But Jasmine had given him good advice during his campaign.

"If you are not sure of someone's name, do not guess at it," she said. "If you make a mistake, it will hurt their feelings and they certainly will not vote for you."

So Melvin was not going to approach the woman – but she came over to him and said, "Hello Melvin."

"Well, I had to say something and since she had just lost her husband, I wanted to say something appropriate," Melvin said. "So I said, 'How are things going?'"

To Melvin, it appeared that the woman was about to cry. So he felt confident that this was Frank Harber's widow.

"I am so sorry about the loss of your husband," Melvin said.

"Thank you, Melvin," she said, patting him on the shoulder. "It has been 25 years now."

"I never found out if I got her vote," Melvin said.

Melvin won the election but remained close friends with his opponent.

During the same years that Melvin served as mayor, 1975-1979, David Boren was governor of Oklahoma.

"During those four years, a lot of good things happened to Seminole — things that I had nothing to do with," Melvin said. "But because I was mayor, I got credit for them. So it would be fair to say that I was the luckiest mayor in Oklahoma."

He met many well-known political people, including Tom Steed of Shawnee, who represented Seminole in Congress for many years.

Seminole had been in the Fourth Congressional District;

after re-districting, the town went into the Third District and was represented by Congressman Carl Albert.

"I had never met Carl Albert, so I sent him a brief letter saying that I was a resident of Seminole and was pleased and proud to be represented by him," Melvin said.

He received a response from Carl Albert, thanking him for his letter. Melvin knew that Congressman Albert had many staff persons working for him and that the letter was probably written by one of them instead of the congressman.

But two years later, he met Congressman Albert at a rally and fundraiser in the Bowlegs football stadium.

"I emphasize that this was in Bowlegs and not in Seminole," Melvin said. "I was one of about 2,000 persons who attended."

As Melvin lined up for his barbecue plate, Congressman Albert started at the head of the line and he greeted and shook the hand of all 2,000 persons. When he came to Melvin, Melvin introduced himself, saying, "I am Melvin Moran. I am pleased to meet you."

The Congressman immediately knew who he was and thanked Melvin again for the "nice letter" he had sent years earlier.

"I was absolutely amazed," Melvin said. "After all, this letter had been written a year or two previously and we were not even in Seminole. But he remembered and I was truly impressed."

Congressman Albert later became Speaker of the House. His chief of staff was Charley Ward, who became Boren's chief of staff when Albert left Congress.

"Once Charley told me he was in Carl Albert's office when Carl Albert was on the telephone with Congressman Steed,"

Melvin said. "Congressman Steed was obviously giving Carl Albert a hard time and Carl seemed troubled and discouraged about the conversation.

"Charley said, 'Congressman Steed can be very difficult sometimes, can't he?'

"With that, Carl Albert became very indignant and said, 'Charley, I don't want you to ever say anything negative about any Oklahoma congressman again.'"

Melvin was one of several individuals who each gave $10,000 to purchase land for Seminole's new hospital.

Mayor Melvin Moran, right, at the end of his term, visited with former Seminole Mayor Gene Price.

Many have asked Melvin what he believed was his most important accomplishment as mayor of Seminole.

"I served on the council for eight years with Fred Adwan as mayor and I believe that his most important accomplishment was the acquisition of Sportsman's Lake," Melvin said.

"I was vice mayor during the six years that Waldo Lilly was mayor. I think his most important accomplishment was the new charter for Seminole. We went from strong mayor form of government to a city manager form of government. Also, while Waldo was mayor, Seminole Junior College was saved [from threatened closing] and our city government certainly had a part in making that happen.

"As to what my most important accomplishment was, other people have more insight that I do," Melvin continued. "But while I was mayor, the entire community was working together — the city government, the Chamber of Commerce, the public school system, the college, and the Seminole Industrial Foundation.

"I think that was the key to the progress that Seminole made during those years and afterwards."

Newspaper accounts of Melvin's tenure as mayor testify to the fact with "Team Effort Builds City," "Seminole Is No. 1 City in State," "Mayor Hails Cooperation," and "City, Chamber Work Together" headlines in *The Seminole Producer* during those years.

One "inconsequential" issue that Melvin was involved in during his years as mayor was the banning of smoking during meetings. During those years, the mayors and many councilors smoked cigars or cigarettes. The council meetings were held in closed up rooms and often lasted four or five hours. By the time they were over, "the smoke would be so thick you could just cut it with a knife," Melvin said. "My clothes were permeated. My wife would say, 'just throw your clothes in the wash before you come in.'"

When he was elected mayor, Melvin prepared carefully for his first meeting. He wrote a thoughtful and in-depth State of the City speech, which included roughly 20 different agenda items. Toward the bottom of the list was a proclamation that from that day forward there would be no more smoking in the council meetings.

"I remember the headline in the papers," Melvin said. "After all the things I had suggested at the meeting, the head-line read, 'Mayor Bans Smoking.'"

Melvin was appointed to serve on the Seminole State College (SSC) Board of Regents by Governor George Nigh in the early 1980s and was reappointed by Governor David Walters.

He served from 1984 to 1997, during which time enroll-ment grew from 1,485 to 1,747. During Melvin's final year as a regent, the SSC board emphasized the need for increased enrollment and set committees and activities in place which resulted in exceeding 2,000 students by the year 2000.

"Seminole State College is one of our major jewels," Melvin said. "The college, founded in 1931, had an average enrollment in the 1960s of 42 students. The Oklahoma State Board of Regents ordered the closure of the college in the late '60s. It's a long but wonderful story. The community in essence said, 'No, we won't.' Today enrollment approaches 2,500 students."

He served during the technology explosion: when the col-lege networked campus computers, set up e-mail campuswide, and created interactive televised instruction capabilities for off-site locations.

They opened the new 13,000-square-foot science wing in Tanner Hall and added 6,000 square feet in the David Boren Library.

During his tenure the name of the college was changed from Seminole Junior College to Seminole State College.

Melvin served under three presidents — Greg Fitch, Dr. Jim Cook, and Dr. Jim Utterback.

"I believe Melvin is the kindest, most genuine, humblest, most generous, faithful, and trustworthy person I have ever known," said Dr. Jim Cook.

"He has become to me a role model of how to live one's life with honor, unselfishness, and service to one's fellow man."

Cook said Melvin helped him and countless others, often when the recipient did not know Melvin was involved.

Jim Utterback remembered the first time he met Melvin Moran; he was one of 20 people interviewing the prospective college president.

"I had been nominated by Carl Albert, who was retired by then, and Glen Johnson, who was Speaker of the House at the time," Utterback said. "We were on the stage at the Jeff Johnston auditorium, 20 people and me in a chair off by myself.

"Melvin had apparently taken a liking to me, I don't know why, and had set me up with what I thought was a leading question. He asked me, 'Do you think your political connections can help Seminole State College?'

"I said 'yes' and was able to talk about state funding."

Utterback believes that Melvin's question, which allowed

him to state some positive facts about the men who had nominated him, may have helped him secure the position.

After being hired, Melvin showed the new president around Seminole and has been a mentor ever since.

"You know, the average job duration for college presidents is about three and a half years," said Utterback, who has served in his position for more than 10 years.

"I attribute a lot of my survival, not to mention my successes, to Melvin. If there is a major issue, it's him I've gone to for advice. When I'm frustrated, he puts me back on track. He's so good at bringing everyone back to being positive.

"I've had hundreds of e-mails complimenting me on something I've done or some success of the college. If there's anything in the newspaper, he e-mails to say how proud he is of us.

"And you know he's probably doing the same thing for everybody else in town – and this isn't something done by a secretary. He has to do it himself."

Utterback showed an e-mail from Melvin he had saved from July of 2006 about some issue he had had with SEDC.

"This e-mail meant a lot to me and is a symbol of the guidance I've come to count on from Melvin," he said, and quoted, " 'And, Jim, when I am angry, hurt, slighted, and 'done wrong,' I have some very bad feelings and some bad thoughts that go through my head. And then I will say to myself, 'Melvin, you are better than they are. And good people do not hold grudges. And now you need to get over [whatever happened] and try to figure out what you can do that will be good and positive for our community.' Jim, I truly feel that way and believe that.'"

Utterback is one of those who say they have never heard

Melvin say anything negative.

"Once when he was trying to make peace over some issue, Melvin said, 'I told him his actions were divisive – that's the word I used, divisive,'" Utterback said. "There's never anything harsher."

Jim Cook had a similar story.

"The harshest criticism of another by Melvin that I ever extracted was in regards to a public figure that was uniformly detested by many of my colleagues," he said. "I knew that Melvin knew the person and asked him one time what he thought of the man.

"In a smiling and understated manner, he simply said, 'The most arrogant man I ever met.' I guess that's pretty harsh criticism from Melvin, since he is the antithesis of arrogance. He has so many characteristics that make him a great leader," Cook said.

Utterback thinks of Melvin often when he reads the speeches of great people and when reading what people saw in great leaders. In fact, he said it would not be an exaggeration to say that anything good happening in Seminole, or maybe in the state, Melvin is promoting it behind the scenes.

Utterback is another, like Robert Henry, who says he has learned a lot about the Jewish faith from Melvin.

"For awhile I was reading about the Holocaust and books of Jewish stories," Utterback said.

"I learned that the Talmud teaches people to look at the positive side. I've only read about it, don't really know the teaching, but from what I've seen, I've often thought that Melvin exemplifies that kind of life," he said.

Pauline Martin, who served on the SSC board with Melvin for several years said Melvin is the most remarkable man she's ever known. "Once, while I was chairman, there was an incident where I was very upset with fellow Regent Ted Phillips," she said. "Everybody else was mad at him, too, and at one point I completely lost my temper."

She asked Melvin how she could go on working with the man.

"You just do," Melvin told her. "You just go on conducting business like you always have in the past and let it go."

"And he was right; that's exactly what I did," Martin said.

Public servants are frequently invited to speak to civic clubs and organizations in Seminole and Melvin's first time to speak to the Lions Club has lived forever in his memory. He had six weeks notice, and spent the time writing and preparing his remarks.

The meeting was held in Seminole's old Harvest House restaurant. Melvin arrived and worked his way through the buffet line and into the meeting room. He sat at the head table with the officers and program chair. After the lunch, the program chairman gave a flowery and flattering introduction.

"It was one of those introductions whereby the speaker normally would get up and say something like, 'That introduction was so flattering I didn't know he was talking about me,'" Melvin said.

The program chairman went on and on and on and the more he talked, the more Melvin thought, "That sure doesn't sound like me." Finally the chairman said, "And our speaker today is…" And it was not Melvin.

"I had come a week early," Melvin said. "So the next 30 minutes I sat there at the head table and tried to make myself invisible. It sure took a lot of guts to come back the next week."

In 1970 he was asked to make a speech at the Presbyterian Church. Prior to the speech there was a reception in the basement of the church. Melvin said he was especially thirsty that evening and the punch was especially delicious.

"I kept going back for refills," he said. "I had no idea that the punch was spiked with alcohol. I made my speech and Jasmine later told me that I spoke somewhat incoherently."

Melvin's feeling about Seminole can be summed up in one story.

"One day I was at the Denver airport," he said. "The woman seated next to me asked where I was from and I said Oklahoma.

"I asked where she was from and she said Colorado.

"I asked in what city she lived and she said she didn't live in a city, but a 'town of about 22,000.'

"I said, 'I live in Seminole. It has 7,000 people – and it's a city.'"

Melvin's politics became well-known in Seminole County and throughout the state. His father, in particular, was very proud of his son's accomplishments, always introducing Melvin as "my son, Melvin, the mayor of Seminole."

"It was as if 'mayor of Seminole' was my last name," Melvin said. "Each time I would feel a little embarrassed, but I never let my Dad know because he was so proud."

Melvin's father died in his Tulsa office in 1979 of lung cancer and a heart attack. Melvin was away in Europe when it happened.

In 1970, the Morans bought a lot at 2300 Morningside Drive. In 1974, they built a house on the property. Their neighbors to the south were Jimmie and Marie Austin, the Seminole oilman who had backed Melvin's campaign for mayor.

The Austins were ardent Republicans and the Morans were committed Democrats. During each election cycle, the Austins would put a sign in their yard proclaiming their support for a Republican candidate. The following day, the Morans would put up a sign for the Democratic opponent. A day or so later, the Austins would put up two signs for other Republican candidates, which would be followed by two Democratic signs in the Moran yard.

"Every Austin sign was countered by a Moran sign during election cycle after election cycle," Melvin said. "Finally the Austins stopped putting up signs. So did the Morans.

"In retrospect, it was all pretty silly," Melvin said, smiling. "We both lived at the end of a street and there was virtually no traffic. During the period of dueling signs,

Melvin rode a donkey during the 1979 Seminole Lazy Days parade.

Melvin and Jasmine visited with Senator John Glenn and his wife, Anne, during their 1979 trip to Oklahoma.

almost no one saw the signs other than the mailman and the newspaper delivery person."

From time to time the Austins supported Democratic candidates, David Boren for example, and the Morans supported Republican candidates, including Wes Watkins. However a Democratic sign was never seen in the Austin yard and a Republican sign was never seen in the Moran yard.

In about 1979, Melvin served as Seminole County campaign manager for George Nigh's bid for governor. Occasionally, the county managers would all meet in Oklahoma City for a pep talk by Nigh and his state campaign chair John Reed.

The same year, Senator John Glenn was considering a run for president. He was scheduled to give a speech in Oklahoma City. Senator David Boren and his wife Molly were going up for the speech and asked Melvin and Jasmine to join them.

"As we were going into the building where Senator Glenn would speak, I saw John Reed from a distance," Melvin said. "He signaled for me to come over and I did."

Reed asked Melvin if he was chauffeuring Senator Boren.

"My answer was, 'no, he's chauffeuring me,'" Melvin laughed. "I may or may not have acquired additional respect that day."

CHAPTER FOURTEEN

Balancing Private and Professional

"You don't realize how precious your time is. People in Europe don't take life so seriously. We needed downtime."

— Jasmine Moran

The years passed quickly because the Morans kept so busy. In addition to Melvin's public service, he and Jasmine bowled in a league on Friday nights.

One morning, Jasmine said, "Mel, I think you are trying to do too much. You have to learn to say no."

That night during their bowling league, a voice on the intercom called Melvin to a phone call. The call from Seminole businessman K.D. Emerick was to inform Melvin that he had just been elected to the board of directors for First Federal Savings and Loan.

"I remembered what Jasmine had said to me that morning and, as I was talking, I could see Jasmine hand-signaling me to please hurry because it was my turn to bowl," Melvin said.

Melvin told Emerick that he could not accept the offer. Emerick used the one statement he thought might change Melvin's mind, "When your father hears what you have just done, he will be ashamed of you." But still Melvin said no.

When he told Jasmine about the call, she said she thought he had made a mistake. "Being on the board of a financial institute is prestigious," she said. "And they probably pay you for attending the meetings. I think you should call them and tell them you have changed your mind."

But Melvin said he could not; the board called him during their meeting and no doubt would already have chosen someone else.

A few years later, Melvin was invited to join the board of directors for First National Bank of Seminole, and said yes "before they had an opportunity to change their minds."

The Morans' social lives included square dancing and playing cards.

"We had a wonderful square dancing group," Jasmine said. "Melvin was a bit hard to pull around, but once we got him headed in the right direction, he did fine. And he enjoyed it, too."

Melvin and Jasmine, second row left, took square dancing classes in the late 1950s.

They played canasta and bridge with several groups, and often with Dr. George Davis and his wife. Their longtime, dearest friends were Isla Mae and Junior Phillips. Isla Mae always accompanied Jasmine musically at auditions and Junior served as Melvin's campaign chairman when he ran for mayor.

Jasmine performed in theaters in Shawnee and in Oklahoma City. One highlight during the early 1980s was Shawnee Little Theater's "A Man for All Seasons," the story of Sir Thomas More. There she performed with Gerald Adams, Governor Brad Henry's Chief of Staff. Adams played Everyman who portrays several people, including the jail keeper in the Tower of London where Sir Thomas More is being held. Jasmine played Sir Thomas More's wife.

"I remember this one line she had to say to me," Adams said. "'You stinking, gutter-bred turnkey!' She said it with such venom! Here was the delightful little woman with her English accent saying this, something I can't even imagine her saying anything close to in real life. And it just struck fear in you.

"In fact, she said it with such gusto that Melvin came to me after one rehearsal to apologize. He said, 'I hope she's not hurting your feelings.'

"They're such wonderful people."

That play also launched a wonderful friendship with Robert Henry, who played Sir Thomas More's son. "It was such an interesting way to meet and get to know each other," said Henry. "Jasmine is a remarkably accomplished actress and singer."

Throughout their years, the kids took up most of Melvin's and Jasmine's time.

"When the kids were little, I was working very long hours,

so most of the credit for the way they've turned out must go to Jasmine," Melvin has said several times.

Jasmine remembered those days when Melvin was on the well servicing unit as a kind of tug-of-war.

"Mel's father was wonderful, but he thought work should come first and life after that," she said. "I was different. When Mel came home on Friday nights, he might have been working 24 hours or, if there was a pulling unit, maybe 36 hours. He'd be exhausted and all he'd want was to get to bed. But I didn't want my children to grow up without knowing their father like I did. I'd find places I thought might be fun to visit and we'd leave as soon as he got home. We'd be gone all weekend, visiting places like Robber's Cave or Woolaroc. We'd take an ice chest and eat on the way. I'd have to drive so he could sleep."

When they got home on Sunday nights, Melvin's father would have been calling all weekend. "Mel struggled between his Dad and me, but I won the weekends," Jasmine said. "I had to be crafty, though. Later it got harder and I had to be craftier.

"You don't realize how precious your time is. People in Europe don't take life so seriously. We needed downtime."

Both Jasmine and Melvin say that she was the disciplinarian of the family.

"I was pretty strict with the children," Jasmine said.

Once, after the first six weeks of school, Marilyn came home crying. Jasmine begged her to tell her what was wrong. "I can't tell you, you'll be so mad," Marilyn said.

"She was all wet from crying," Jasmine said. "Finally I got her to tell me. Sobbing, she said she had gotten a B on her six weeks paper.

"I told her, if I brought home a B, Granny would have had a celebration for everyone. We never had that problem again."

Jasmine's mother was her inspiration. "She was as tough as nails and if you crossed her, you'd better hide," Jasmine said. "I spent plenty of time hiding in a closet. She said, 'You know you'll have to come out sometime.' But I always let her cool off first. She had a very strong conscience and I was born with one, too."

The Morans decided that if they were going to stay in Seminole, they would get involved in the community.

"We wanted to meet people and find ways to improve ourselves and the town," Jasmine said.

Mel had his community service and Jasmine had the PTA and social sororities.

"Joanne Parker was leader of the Bluebirds and I was her assistant," she remembered.

During their children's high school years, Jasmine and Melvin were active with the Seminole High School (SHS) debate team, driving them to meets.

"They didn't have a bus for the team then, so parents took them," she said. "Sometimes Melvin would be taking them in one direction and I'd be taking them in another."

Melvin's support of the high school debate team began long before his children were on the team.

"The father of modern day Seminole may have been Harland B. Mitchell, the speech and debate instructor at Seminole High School and Seminole Junior College for 35 years," Melvin said.

"During the 20th century, no school in America had more

national speech and debate champions than Seminole High School. For appropriate reasons, the national forensics trophy was named the H.B. Mitchell."

Mitchell's students included Oklahoma Governor, United States Senator and University of Oklahoma President David Boren, former United States House of Representative Speaker Jim Wright, and the Today Show's first host, Frank McGee. Hundreds of his students have become educators, political leaders, attorneys, ministers, and television anchors. They helped build Seminole and Oklahoma and many have had a national influence.

One of those debate students who represented SHS well through his life was former United States Senator David Boren. Boren was 14 and in junior high school. "My family was acquainted with the Morans," Boren said. "Melvin's coming back to Seminole with a British bride was big news — there weren't many actresses in Seminole. Everyone got to know them quickly.

"They took an interest in high school debaters and student leaders; I was class president," Boren continued. "They made an impression on me as a teen. I was able to talk to her about Britain and him about the war. They took time to have conversations with me and talk about experiences.

"I remember going to see Jasmine perform in community theater when I was in high school. Melvin would come to debate classes and give critiques and helpful advice. They came to school often. Later, in law school, we continued to have conversations."

H.B. Mitchell, who inspired more than a generation of high school students, left Seminole in 1968, but Marilyn Moran was in his class in eighth grade. The Morans' children could be counted among those who have carried Seminole schools' influence far and wide.

"Jasmine and I both agree that our greatest achievement has been our children," Melvin said. "We have really been blessed in so many ways.

"Our three children have all been high achievers," he continued. "The achievements and honors that each has received have far exceeded anything that I may have done."

Oldest daughter Marilyn attended Purdue University and received her degree in communications. She had a seven-year career as a television news anchor, working first in Lafayette, Indiana, then in Fort Myers, Florida, and then in Fort Wayne, Indiana.

In Lafayette, she married her co-anchor, Bill Townsend. They co-anchored together in Fort Myers and Fort Wayne. Both quit their jobs and formed CVC Communications, which produces videos and meetings all over the world for large corporations.

"Bill is one of the kindest persons anyone could ever have as a son-in-law," Melvin said.

Marilyn was the first female elected as chair of the Indiana State Chamber of Commerce. When she was selected as Indiana Woman of the Year, her parents were there to see her accept the honor. "We were so proud," Melvin said.

Elisa attended the University of Indiana and received her degree in communications as well. She attended the University of Colorado and received her law degree. While in law school, she met and married another law student, Gary Kleiman.

"I had always hoped that one of my children would come

into our family business and become my successor," Melvin said. "And Gary fulfilled my dream by doing that. Though he is a lawyer in Denver, he co-manages our family oil company."

Elisa has a thriving law practice in Denver and is involved in civic activities.

"When she was selected as the Denver Jewish Woman of the Year, we were at the banquet along with 1,000 other people," Melvin said. "And we were so proud."

For as long as Melvin and Jasmine can remember, their son, David, wanted to be a physicist, and hoped to work for NASA. He received his degree in physics from the University of Michigan and was awarded a two-year scholarship to study at Cambridge University in England. He then worked toward his doctorate degree in physics while teaching physics at Cornell University.

"At that point in his life, David changed his mind and went back to Michigan and earned a law degree," Melvin said. For more than 15 years he worked in the Appellate Division of the Public Defenders Office for the state of Michigan. For several years, he was a law professor and associate dean of the law school in Detroit. David has argued cases before the United States Supreme Court on five occasions.

Melvin was present for four of those occasions and Jasmine was present on his first three visits to the Supreme Court.

Melvin vividly remembers his son's first argument at the court, during which David said, "With all due respect, Justice Scalia, what you have just said was not accurate." David followed up with his explanation of why.

"At that moment, my thought was, 'I can't believe my

During the early 2000s, the Moran clan gathered on the steps of the Supreme Court during one of the five times son David argued cases before the august board.

Melvin and Jasmine are proud grandparents. They celebrated the arrival of the first with new mom Marilyn, daughter Elisa, son David, and son-in-law Bill Townsend, center back.

son said that,'" Melvin said. "And I was so proud of him that I feared the buttons of my shirt would pop off and I hoped they would not make a noise when they landed on the floor."

In September, 2008, David moved to a new position as head of the University of Michigan's Project Innocence program. The national program, with centers in several states, searches for evidence which will allow innocent people to be released from prison. David also continues to teach law at the University of Michigan.

While getting his undergraduate degree in Michigan, David fell in love with Michigan student Kris Olsson. She heads an environmental organization whose goal is to keep Michigan waters clean and free of pollution.

"Kris has been a wonderful wife for David and a wonderful mother for two of our granddaughters," Melvin said.

"As proud as we are regarding our children's achievements, Jasmine and I are prouder because of the type of persons our children have become," Melvin said. "They deeply care about other people and they do everything they possibly can to make the world a better place."

Also figuring among the Morans' immediate family are their six granddaughters.

Marilyn and Bill have two daughters, Allison and Julie.

"Allison always wanted to work in the medical field," Melvin said. "She spent a lot of time working in emergency rooms and as an EMT on ambulances. Jasmine and I have never been prouder of her than when she spent some time in Africa taking care of the sick."

Allison is presently a pharmaceutical representative, and married to pediatrician, Dr. Aaron Sackett.

"In our family, there are many lawyers, but we always wanted a doctor," Melvin said. "And we have welcomed Aaron into our family."

Julie is "a very caring person," according to her grandfather.

In college she majored in social work and in Spanish. After graduation, she went to work for the YMCA in Chile. With a salary of less than $100 a week, Julie loved her job. While in Chile, she fell in love with the YMCA manager. They married and live in Fort Wayne where Julie works for a university.

"Her husband's name is Panchito and he is one of the sweetest people anyone could ever know," Melvin said. "Just before their marriage, Panchito went to his future father-in-law, Bill Townsend, and said, 'You do not have any sons to carry on your name, so I will change my name to Townsend.'"

Elisa and Gary have two daughters, Michelle and Nicole.

Michelle is a student at the University of Michigan and Nicole is a high school student in Denver.

"When a Jewish boy turns 13, and after many years of study, he will have a Bar Mitzvah," Melvin said. "When a Jewish girl turns 13, she will have a Bat Mitzvah.

"When Michelle had her Bat Mitzvah in Denver, Jasmine and I were present as very proud grandparents. For me this was such a joyful occasion that I cried out loud. It was one of the highlights of my life.

Proud grandparents Melvin and Jasmine with granddaughter Nicole on the occasion of her Bat Mitzvah.

"Just before Nicole's Bat Mitzvah, Elisa came to me and said, 'Dad, please don't cry this time.' I unsuccessfully tried to comply. But again, Jasmine and I were so proud."

David and Kris also have two daughters, Annika, seven, and Ingrid, five.

"They are adorable and intelligent and we know we will receive equal joy and pride from our two youngest grand-daughters," Melvin said.

"Dad is a guy completely dedicated to serving his com-munity and the people around him," David said. "He is defi-nitely my role model. I don't live up to what he's done in public service, but I try.

"If nothing else, he instilled in us an awareness that there are many people not as fortunate as we are and I try to pass this on to my daughters. They're still young, but I want them to have an understanding of the obligation to give back to the community.

"I remember as a boy, Dad's insistence that we go to see how people live who weren't doing as well as we were, visiting the worst parts of town to see how other people live. In Semi-nole, he started the Rotary Club's Christmas dinner for people who couldn't afford one. We served people who had rags for clothing and hadn't seen a dentist in many years.

"We saw how fortunate we were. I had that obligation instilled in me completely. That's the kind of guy he is."

On religion, David said his parents encouraged open mindedness and curiosity.

"A lot of religious people demand that their children fol-low their religion," David said. "Dad encouraged us to look for answers. I questioned religious doctrine at an early age. He

The Moran clan in Jasmine Moran Children's Museum t-shirts in 1989.

introduced me to the Talmud, which stresses ethical require-
ments and that has been very influential in the way I developed
my own personal philosophy.

"I am not particularly religious, but I follow Jewish ethics,
Jewish obligations to my fellow man, whether they are Jewish
or not."

Marilyn's husband was Christian and, when their children arrived, they had to choose which religion to follow; they
settled on the Christian religion.

Asked if he was disappointed by his daughter's choice not
to follow the religion that is so important to him, Melvin said,
"Yes, but I understood. It is her life and I always wanted our
children to be independent."

CHAPTER FIFTEEN

Life with the Good Humor Man

"Okay, Ms. Hill, I will call Radio Shack and call you back."

— Melvin Moran

The 1960s and 1970s rushed by the Morans with events both historical and hilarious.

In the 1960s, the Morans had an opportunity to visit Israel and to meet for the first time Melvin's relatives who still live in the Tel Aviv area. Only one of the relatives, Inna, the daughter of Melvin's first cousin, Mordecai Druyan, spoke English.

Melvin called her home and found Inna to speak fluent English. They made plans that someone would pick them up at their hotel at 7:00 p.m. But after they hung up, Jasmine wondered if that meant before or after dinner.

"Jasmine and I agreed that we did not want the family to go to the trouble of making dinner for us," Melvin said. Jasmine urged him to call Inna back and tell her they would eat dinner at the hotel before being picked up.

When he called back Inna was no longer there. All the remaining family members spoke Hebrew, Russian, and Yiddish. Yiddish is slang German and most of the Jews of Europe spoke Yiddish. When Melvin was growing up as a child in Seminole, his paternal grandmother lived with them and spoke very poor English. Meyer and Elsie both spoke to her in Yiddish.

"I have never ever spoken a word of Yiddish, but after hearing it in my home so frequently, I could understand quite a lot of it," Melvin said. So he attempted to communicate with his family in Yiddish.

"I put Yiddish words together as best I could and said, I thought, 'You are going to pick us up at our hotel at 7:00 p.m. We will go ahead and eat at 6:00 p.m.,'" Melvin said.

But it was interpreted as "7:00 p.m. is too late for us to eat. We wish to eat at 6:00 p.m."

"Boy, what an ugly American I must have seemed!" Melvin said. The family had rushed their food preparations and had dinner ready at 6:00 p.m.

"They served us a wonderful meal and it was a wonderful, loving evening," Melvin said.

One of Melvin's family members was a shoe manufacturer — what Melvin called a "very low-tech shoe manufacturer." He had a small factory, only about 700 square feet, and he invited Melvin to visit. He asked Melvin what size shoe he wore — in Yiddish, because that was their only common language.

"It was obvious to me that he wanted to give me a pair of shoes," Melvin said. "I knew that he was struggling and I did not want to accept shoes without paying for them. I tried to find the right Yiddish words to tell him that I could not accept a pair of shoes unless he allowed me to pay him, but I simply could not find the right words. I showed him the only way that I could think of, by taking out my billfold, which was black, and pointing to it."

His family member said, 'Oh, you would like a pair of black shoes?"

"I said no and took some bills out of my billfold," Melvin said. "Then he said in Yiddish, 'I understand; you would like a pair of green shoes?'

"He did give me a beautiful pair of shoes and he would not accept money for them. I still have those shoes and I treasure them."

Israel continued to play a special part in Melvin's life. Because of his relationship with Israel and some of Israel's government officials, he had a visit in 1979 from the former Israeli Ambassador Yaakov Avnon who was serving as Director of Protocol at the Israel Ministry of Foreign Affairs. The ambassador stayed for several days with Melvin and Jasmine in their Seminole home.

In 1979, Melvin had an opportunity to visit with Israeli President Yitzhak Navon, left. The meeting came about with the help of Israel Ambassador Yaakov Avnon, center.

One day Avnon told Melvin that Yitzhak Navon, president of Israel, was coming to New York City after meeting with the President of the United States. The ambassador asked Melvin if he would like to go and meet with him.

"I believe he was making an effort to repay our hospitality," Melvin said. "It's not often that one has an opportunity to meet a president, so I responded that I would very much like to do that."

Avnon made a phone call and told Melvin to fly to New York on Tuesday and check into a specific hotel. For security reasons, he was to tell no one where he was. On Wednesday morning at 11:00 a.m., Melvin was told to go down to the lobby, where Israeli security would meet him near the elevator and escort him to the room of the president.

Avnon warned Melvin to "stay in your room from 10:00 a.m. to 11:00 a.m. Israeli security might call you and give you the room number of the president. If that happens, proceed directly to the room."

On Tuesday Melvin flew to New York, checked into the hotel and told no one. On Wednesday morning at 10:30 a.m., his phone rang.

"Since no one knew where I was, this had to be Israeli security giving me the president's room number," Melvin said.

Actually, it was a hotel guest dialing a Manhattan phone number. He forgot to dial "9" to get an outside line. When he dialed the first three numbers, 516, Melvin's phone rang because that was his room number. So while Melvin thought he was talking to Israeli security, the hotel guest thought he was speaking to the hotel operator.

"Hello," Melvin answered the phone.

"Five-one-six," said the voice at the other end, giving his number to whom he thought was the hotel operator.

"Yes," Melvin said, interrupting.

"One two six eight," said the voice, continuing.

"One moment please," Melvin said as he put down the phone and walked across the room for a pen so he could write down the president's room number.

"One two six eight," Melvin repeated as he wrote down the number. The voice at the other end said, "Yes."

"Would you like me to proceed directly to the room?" Melvin asked.

After a moment of silence, the voice on the other end asked, "Why would I want you to do that?"

"Then should I go downstairs by the elevator?" Melvin asked.

"Why would you go down to the elevator?" the voice asked.

"Then what would you like me to do?" Melvin asked, somewhat exasperated.

"I want you to dial the number," the voice said.

Melvin thought to himself, "I am not supposed to call the president, I am supposed to see him." So he asked, "Why would I do that?"

The other voice said, "Isn't this the hotel operator?"

Melvin said, "No" and hung up.

"At 11:00 a.m. I did go to the lobby and I did meet with the president," Melvin said.

Melvin had a private meeting with Israeli President Navon for thirty minutes in his room and described it as "a great experience."

Melvin has been able to meet many famous and interesting people during his lifetime, including Jane Jayroe, while she served as Miss America.

In 1967, Miss America Jane Jayroe was a guest at the Miss Seminole pageant, organized by Melvin and Jasmine Moran.

Melvin and Jasmine chaired the Rotary Club-sponsored Miss Seminole pageant throughout the 1960s.

Jayroe was Miss Oklahoma when she earned the title of Miss America, so Melvin contacted the Miss America office to see if she might participate in the Miss Seminole pageant. He was sent an application with rules and restrictions.

"Among other things, Miss America is only allowed to work four hours each day," Melvin said. "And every appearance, no matter how short, counts as one hour."

They sent in an application stating that Miss America would appear at the Miss Seminole pageant for two hours, she would be in a parade that afternoon for one hour and she would be asked to a tea for contestants and mothers for another hour that afternoon.

"Miss America coming to Seminole was a big deal," Melvin said. During the months before she came, almost every organization in town contacted the Morans to see if Miss America could do something with them while she was there. To each request, he explained the four-hour time limit, but added, "I will ask Jane if she could do that."

One friend, Bill Parks, came to Melvin's office and asked if he could get Miss America to sign photos for his two grand-daughters and Melvin said he would. During the next several months, Bill contacted Melvin almost weekly to remind him of the autographed pictures. The day before Jane arrived, Bill came in to remind him and Melvin said, "Don't worry, Bill, I won't forget."

At 10:00 a.m. on the day of the pageant, Miss America arrived and the Morans checked her into a motel so she could rest between events.

"However, almost as soon as she arrived, I started mentioning some of these other requests from other organizations," Melvin said. "To each one, she graciously said, 'Of course, I would be happy to do that.'

"From the time she arrived at about 10:00 a.m.

During her visit to Seminole, Miss America Jane Jayroe was introduced to "Phyllis Diller," played in the skit by Jasmine Moran.

until our pageant ended that evening about 11:00 p.m., she never rested at all. She was so willing to do everything."

The pageant was a huge success. During intermission Miss America even went into the audience and visited. "She could not have been more gracious," Melvin said.

About 10 minutes before the pageant ended, Melvin remembered Bill Parks' granddaughters. Melvin had difficulty trying to get up the nerve to ask her to do one more thing, after all she had done all day. So Melvin told a little white lie.

"Jane, during intermission, a man came over to me and said his two granddaughters were in the hospital and he thought it would help them recover if they could have auto-graphed pictures of you addressed to them," Melvin said.

Jayroe, gracious as always, responded with, "Of course, I would be happy to do that. Melvin, do you think I should say, 'get well soon' or 'I wish you a speedy recovery?"

"How about best wishes?" Melvin said.

Jayroe and the Morans have been good friends ever since. He said he considered it a privilege to work with her again when he was appointed to the Tourism Commission in 2003, while she was serving as director.

In the mid '60s, Jasmine and Melvin took a trip to Ger-many to visit Jasmine's sister, Davina Skedzuhn, in Frankfurt. A week before they were to leave, there was a story in the local newspaper stating that Germany was minting several new gold coins, which had a likeness of President Kennedy on them. Several coin collector friends asked Melvin to purchase some of these coins for their collections and Melvin agreed.

But at the German bank, Melvin was told the coins were

not kept in stock. It would take a week to receive them and Melvin had to leave before they would arrive.

"The bank official said they had some silver Kennedy coins, and I felt my coin collector friends would be delighted to have these, so I told the bank official that I would like 30 of them," Melvin said.

He paid for them with German currency, about 80 cents each.

"I didn't examine them until after I left the bank," Melvin said. "At that time, I discovered I had paid 80 cents each for American Kennedy half dollars. I was too embarrassed to take them back."

With his sense of humor and his dedication to community, Melvin quickly became a much-sought-after speaker for local banquets, meetings, and reunions. One of his favorite humorous, but completely true, stories was about his 1972 purchase of a little green telephone for David's room.

They bought the phone at Radio Shack in Crossroads Mall in Oklahoma City and were reminded by the salesman, whose nametag said Roger, that they needed to notify Southwestern Bell that they were installing a new phone. The Federal Trade Commission (FTC) registration number would be on the box.

The next day, Melvin called the Seminole Southwestern Bell office and gave them the registration number, then threw away the box.

But the next day, he received a call from the Southwestern Bell district office.

"Yes, Mrs. Hill, I did purchase an additional telephone... I already gave the FTC registration number to your Seminole office… No, Mrs. Hill, I do not understand why you are required to get the number directly from the customer. I cannot give it to you because it was on the box and I threw away the box…You say the store where we purchased the phone will have that number on record? Mrs. Hill, we purchased the phone at Radio Shack in Oklahoma City. I will call them, get the number and call you back."

Melvin called Radio Shack and asked to speak to Roger.

"Roger, this is Melvin Moran in Seminole. On Tuesday afternoon my wife and I purchased a cute little green telephone from you…Roger, my wife was the lady with the English accent… Yes, Roger, I will give her your regards. Roger, Southwestern Bell needs the FTC registration number…Yes, Roger, I know it was on the box. But I threw away the box after giving the number to the local Southwestern Bell office."

Roger said he could get the number from Ed, the store manager.

"Roger, Southwestern Bell said they also need the ringer exchange number and the O.C.O.C. code number."

Roger asked Melvin to hold on, which Melvin did for about 15 minutes.

"I calculated that the cost of this phone call cost me more than I had paid for that stupid green phone," Melvin said.

But when Roger came back, Melvin said, "No, Roger, that's perfectly okay. I do not mind holding at all."

Roger gave Melvin an 11-digit FTC registration number and a seven-digit ringer exchange number and said the O.C.O.C. code was RJ11.

Melvin called back to Mrs. Hill at Southwestern Bell.

"Mrs. Hill, I spoke to Radio Shack and here are the numbers

they gave me…What's that, Mrs. Hill? All three of the numbers are wrong? The FTC registration number must be 14 digits and I only gave you 11? The ringer exchange number is completely wrong? And the O.C.O.C. code number is incomplete? Okay, Ms. Hill, I will call Radio Shack and call you back."

Melvin phoned again to the Radio Shack in Oklahoma City. "Roger, this is Melvin Moran in Seminole again. Southwestern Bell said the numbers you gave me were wrong. You gave me an 11-digit FTC registration number and it needs to be 14 digits. So I need three more digits. Roger, I don't care what three numbers you give me. And I need an altogether different ringer exchange number and she said the RJ11 code number was incomplete."

Roger went back to Ed for more numbers. He came back with three more digits for the FTC registration number and a new ringer exchange number, but he said Ed, the store manager, said the RJ11 code number was correct. Melvin returned his call to Southwestern Bell.

"Mrs. Hill, I have new numbers from Radio Shack." This time she said the FTC registration number was correct and that the new ringer exchange number was also correct. But Ms. Hill said that RJ11 was incomplete because the number had to be either RJ11 W or RJ11 C.

"Mrs. Hill, I will call Radio Shack and I will call you back."

"By this time, I was looking upon Roger as a good friend," said Melvin.

"Hi, Rog, this is Mel. Melvin Moran. Melvin Moran from Seminole. The guy with the wife with the accent… Yes, Roger, I will give her your regards. Rog, Mrs. Hill said the O.C.O.C.

code number must be RJ11 W or RJ11 C."

Roger said, "Tell her W."

"Mrs. Hill, Radio Shack said the phone number was RJ11 W… What's that, Mrs. Hill? You want to know if the phone hangs on the wall or sits on the desk? Well, Mrs. Hill, it sits on the desk." Mrs. Hill said that if it sits on the desk, it could not be RJ11 W because W stands for wall.

"Well, then Mrs. Hill, it must be RJ11 C."

"Mrs. Hill said she could not accept that from me because it must come directly from the store. So I called Radio Shack and Roger said that he would call the manufacturer in Fort Worth and call me back the next day.

"That evening, Mrs. Hill called again. She said she had re-read her instructions and discovered that RJ11 was the correct O.C.O.C. code number after all. I thanked her and then she asked me about the cord on the telephone. I said, 'Well, Mrs. Hill, it's a thin gray cord about six feet long. At the end of the cord there is a plastic module. And I purchased an adapter from Radio Shack to go from module to the four-pronged wall jack.

"What's that, Mrs. Hill? You need the FTC registration number of that adapter? I will call Radio Shack and I will call you back."

"And I did."

Melvin's deadpan presentation and his timing — allowing just enough time so the audience knew what he was really thinking about Mrs. Hill's requests — never failed to rouse audiences to waves of hysterical laughter, proving that you can send the comedy writer to business school, but deep down, he will remain a comedian all his life.

CHAPTER SIXTEEN

The Golf Pro

"I wonder how good you have to be to NOT be kicked off St. Andrews."
— Ron Moddelmog

    Melvin is never funnier than when on the golf course — or talking about golf.

    "I played golf for the first time when I was about 17 years old and living in Tulsa," he said. "My brother, Sidney, and I played a round of golf together. It was the first time on the golf course for either of us and neither of us knew what we were doing, how to hold a club properly or anything else about the game of golf.

    "When we played that round, we only counted the times we actually hit the ball. There were many more times when we didn't. After 17 holes, I was down by 18 strokes. But by the time we completed the 18th hole, I won the match by 22 strokes. I do not remember what our final scores were, but the scores were in the neighborhood of 350.

    "After that resounding victory my first time out, I was hooked on the game."

    He played off and on for decades.

    "I never took a lesson and acquired many bad habits," Melvin said. "I was a terrible golfer and I often referred to myself as 'the worst golfer in Oklahoma.' Over the years many golfers said to me, 'No, no, you can't possibly be.' But after they play a round of golf with me, they always say, 'Yes, you are.'"

Throughout Melvin's life, he has never used profanity, not even mild curses. It was on the golf course that he developed the expletive, "Oh, Melvin!" which became legendary in Seminole and beyond.

"When I play golf and hit a bad shot, which is most of the time, I say, 'Oh, Melvin!'" he said. "Sometimes if I hit a house or a car, I do get carried away and I exclaim, 'Oh, Melvin, Melvin, Melvin!' That's as strong as my language gets."

Once he played in Seminole with his friend Neal Molleur. That day, as usual, there were a lot of, "Oh, Melvins." If Molleur hit a bad shot, he would use a more traditional curse.

"After we finished our round of golf, Neal said to me, 'Melvin, I admire you. I am going to try to follow the example you have set for me and clean up my language,'" Melvin recalled.

Six months later, Melvin played with a new golf buddy, Chuck Prucha. After a few holes and several "Oh Melvins," Prucha said, "Now I understand."

Prucha explained that he recently had played with Neal Molleur and every time Molleur hit a bad shot, Neal said, "Oh, Melvin!"

In Seminole hearing, "Oh Melvin!" is not uncommon. A number of people are now using it as their bad shot expletive. There are golf balls with "Oh Melvin!" printed on them. Melvin even was presented with an "Oh, Melvin!" shirt.

"It was suggested to me that when I hit a bad shot, I could save my voice and simply point to the lettering on the shirt," Melvin said. "I tried that, but it just wasn't the same. We golfers have a need to verbally express ourselves."

One day Melvin was playing golf with his friend, Vernon Mullen. It was their first golf outing. On the first tee, Melvin's drive was probably the best he had ever hit on that hole.

"I was standing there admiring my shot when Vernon said, 'Melvin, if you like, why don't you go ahead and take a mulligan [do over],'" Melvin said. "That really hurt my feelings. I responded with, 'Vernon, for me, that was as good as it gets.'"

The *piece de resistance* of Melvin's golf stories was the one where he played on the prestigious St. Andrews golf course in Scotland. St. Andrews was the first golf course in the world and is the most revered. The British Open often is played there.

In the 1980s, the Morans took a bus tour of Scotland to seek Jasmine's roots. On the bus, they made friends with a couple from Florida. The man, Lou, was a retired banker. He said he played golf six days a week. He said his goal in life was to play the Old Course at St. Andrews.

The next day the tour took the Morans to Edinborough, which is about 70 miles from St. Andrews. During a free day on the tour, Melvin suggested hiring a car to travel to St. Andrews. Lou loved the idea. The wives could shop while the men played golf...if indeed they were able to get on the course.

"When we arrived at the course, there was a twosome who allowed us to play with them, so we were able to play at the famed St. Andrews," Melvin said.

At St. Andrews there is no such thing as a golf cart. One has to have a caddy. So Melvin and Lou went to the little building where a caddy could be engaged. "To hire a caddy that day cost eight pounds, 10 pounds, or 12 pounds. Melvin asked for a caddy and was given a 12-pound caddy.

"My caddy was a very large man," Melvin said. "I assumed he was a golfer, so I asked him what his average score was. He responded, '72.' That really unnerved me. Here I was a very poor golfer, playing on the most-revered course in the world and I had, like, Jack Nicklaus for my caddy."

Considering his level of ability, Melvin thought he got off to a good start. They completed five holes and were on the sixth green. In the distance, Melvin could see a man walking in their direction. When he was close enough, Melvin could read the words on his t-shirt and on his cap — "Golf Ranger."

He walked directly up to Melvin and said, "I have been watching you play and I don't believe your ability is up to our standards. You need to find someplace else to play."

"And he then ejected me from the course!" Melvin said.

"To think of Melvin, this meticulous, quiet, retiring, nice man, being thrown off the golf course is hilarious," said Gerald Adams. "I imagine it must have been quite embarrassing for him."

But, as usual, Melvin took the story and turned it into a joke on himself.

"As I was being led off the course, my friend Lou was very embarrassed for me," Melvin said. "But he was not about to leave with me. After all, this was his goal in life. Then my caddy said, 'Melvin, no matter how long or how short a round is, we still expect our gratuity.' So I tipped 'Jack.'"

That day Melvin made a promise to himself — when he got home, he would take golf lessons and some day he would return to St. Andrews – and not get kicked off the course.

Back in Seminole, he told the golf pro, "When I complete my lessons, I would like for you to take me out on the course and if I can break 100, I will give you a bonus of $500." While this did give the pro an incentive, and he tried as hard as he could, Melvin never arrived at the point where he said, "Let's see if you can break 100 now."

A few months later Melvin and his friend Harvey McMains were getting ready to tee off on the 13th hole, which is a par three. Not far from the tee is a small lake. The green is on the other side of the lake on top of a high hill.

"Because of my lack of ability, three-quarters of the time my tee shot will go into the lake," Melvin said. "One-quarter of the time my tee shot will land on the hill. I had never hit a ball on the green because I do not hit a golf ball that far."

As he and McMains were getting ready to tee off, the entire Seminole High School boys' golf team stood by, along with their coach, Ron Moddelmog.

As Melvin was getting ready to hit the ball, Moddelmog said to his young golfers, "Be quiet, boys, and watch these golfers. Perhaps you can learn something from them."

"If there was ever pressure on a golfer, well, that was it," Melvin said. "I decided I needed a plan of action. After I would hit my ball into the lake, I decided that I would not look back and see those young boys laughing at me. Instead, I decided that I would keep my eyes straight ahead, go to the other side of the lake, lay my ball on the side of the hill, and then take my second shot.

"Well, I hit my tee shot. It went over the lake. It went over the hill. It landed on the green about 10 feet from the pin.

Obviously I needed a new plan of action," Melvin said. "So I looked back at the boys and tried to look disgusted that I was that far from the pin."

That evening, Moddelmog and McMains ran into each other. Moddelmog had heard the story about Melvin being kicked off St. Andrews. After seeing Melvin play that day, he asked McMains, "I wonder how good you have to be to NOT be kicked off St. Andrews."

At Thanksgiving that same year, Melvin met his children at Breakers Hotel in Miami Beach, Florida.

"I would describe the golf course there as posh," Melvin said. "There were lots of palm trees and it was beautiful."

David and Melvin decided to play a round of golf. While Melvin is used to playing badly, he had never played as badly as he did that day.

"I was miss-hitting almost every shot," Melvin said.

Finally on the seventh tee, he hit his tee shot and it was one of the best tee shots he had ever hit. It went high and far, "almost like a real golfer," Melvin said.

As he went to the ball and prepared to take his second shot, Melvin could see a person in a golf cart coming towards him. The man had a blazer with the golf club's logo on it. Melvin knew it was a golf ranger coming to kick him off the course.

"I was prepared to tell him, 'Sir, I have been kicked off a much nicer course than this one,'" Melvin said.

But the golf ranger had only seen Melvin's last shot.

"He came directly to me and said, 'Sir, on behalf of this golf club, I want to apologize to you for the four duffers who are playing just ahead of you. We never should have let them on this course.'

"I quietly said, 'That's okay. I understand.'"

The story about Melvin's ejection from St. Andrews was passed around internationally. General Tom Kelly, who planned the Desert Storm offensive, was a guest speaker at an Oklahoma Independent Petroleum Association (OIPA) meeting at Shangri La Resort in northeastern Oklahoma. When Melvin was introduced to him, they asked him to tell the St. Andrews story and he did.

The following fall, while Melvin was in Norman for an OU football game, he ran into a Tulsa friend, Curtis Green, who had just returned from a visit to Israel. He said, "Melvin, I bring regards from your friend, General Tom Kelly." Melvin said, "I have met General Kelly, but he would not exactly be a friend."

Green said he attended a reception in Tel Aviv honoring the general, who started his talk by saying, "First I want to tell you a story about a friend of mine and what happened to him at St. Andrews."

So far, Melvin has not improved his game enough to return to St. Andrews as he promised himself after being thrown off that day. But in 2004 at Shangri La Resort for a weekend, he saw the golf pro giving lessons and thought he might give it a try.

"The pro asked me to hit a few golf balls and when I did, he was somewhat complimentary, but he tempered that by saying, 'We need to make some changes,'" Melvin said.

"It so happened that everything I was doing was wrong. He changed my grip, my backswing, my stance, my shoulders, my swing, my follow-through, etcetera. He said there were seven things that I needed to change and he taught them to me in the order that they needed to be done. So I addressed the ball and I first did step one, followed by number two, number three, all the way to number seven."

Melvin hit the ball and it probably went a hundred yards further than he had ever hit a ball in his life. Melvin thought this was just an accident, so after going through the seven steps, he hit a second ball and it went just as far. And then a third and a fourth. He put down the driver and tried hitting the ball with other clubs and was amazed at the positive difference regarding the distance the ball traveled. "However, I wondered if this would translate to hitting the ball well on an actual course," Melvin said.

When he got back to Seminole, Melvin tried the steps on the Jimmie Austin course there.

"As I went through the seven steps, I was amazed," Melvin said. "I was hitting the golf ball like I never imagined I could, like a real golfer hits a golf ball."

During the next six months, Melvin's handicap went down by a full 20 strokes.

"I was so proud," he said. "Then one night, I woke up in the middle of the night and started going through the seven steps. I imagined step number one, number two, number three, and then I came to step number four and I could not remember step number four. I remembered numbers five, six and seven. But I could not remember step number four. I thought that, when I was actually hitting the ball on the golf course that step number four would come back to me," Melvin said. "Well, it didn't. And I soon discovered that if you only do six steps, leaving out number four, you miss the ball entirely."

Melvin was so discouraged. He tried to contact the Shangri La pro, but he had left the state and could not be located. "So I am now back to my old swing and it takes me 20 strokes more to play a round of golf," Melvin lamented.

"He's a terrible golfer," said his high school friend Maynard Ungerman. "I don't know why he keeps playing. I swear I see the golf ball twitch to one side when he approaches, knowing it's about to get sliced."

A few years later Melvin and Jasmine were in San Francisco for the Independent Petroleum Association of America's annual meeting. During a coffee break, two Oklahomans joined them and one told the story of the golfer who was kicked off St. Andrews.

"When he finished, I told him that he was talking about me," Melvin said. "He was so embarrassed, but I loved it."

Years later, when Melvin was inducted into the Oklahoma Hall of Fame, Arnold Palmer was presenting Vince Gill for induction. "I thought shaking his hand might improve my game, but it didn't," Melvin said.

Melvin's friends Marci and Dale Donaho contacted Palmer and asked him to autograph a famous picture of himself on St. Andrews during a British Open tournament. Palmer signed it with a special note just for Melvin. The photo hangs in Melvin's office and is one of his most precious possessions.

Unfortunately golf is not the only area where Melvin finds himself athletically challenged. In about 1990 he enthusiastically agreed to play in a charity basketball game at Seminole State College. A group of local people were invited to play against the Channel 4 news team.

"At one point during the game, I was in the middle of the court," Melvin said. "My feet got tangled up with each other and I fell to the ground. There was not another player within 15 feet of me. As I lay there on the court, I said to myself, 'I hope nobody saw this.' Later I discovered that everybody did."

"All those stories about him being a klutz are true," said his sister, Jeannie Tiras. "He doesn't look where he's going. Once when we were in New York for a reunion, he was talking and stepped off the curb and a bus would have hit him if my husband hadn't pulled him back onto the curb."

CHAPTER SEVENTEEN

How to Survive a Recession

"My decision to purchase United Community stock in 1985 was the single-best financial decision I have ever made."

— Melvin Moran

The 1960s and 1970s were good years for the Morans. The 1980s, however, started off with tough times, before ending with a golden era that will likely give Melvin and Jasmine Moran their place in the history books.

In 1986, the price of oil collapsed. Seminole was in a depression and the state was in a recession. Oil companies were losing money with every barrel of oil they pulled from the ground and many went broke. The Morans were not as impacted, in part because their lifestyle always had been conservative.

"When I first moved to Oklahoma, I thought the worst thing about the people here was that they don't save anything," said Jasmine. "Not newspapers, not animals, not even old people – they just put them in nursing homes. I was foretelling the future. We don't recycle, we just throw everything out. We don't know what it's like to be without. This was hard for me to adjust to. I was used to a stringent budget. If the price went up one cent, I wouldn't buy it. Mel would say, 'We're able to afford it' and I'd say, 'But who knows about tomorrow?'

"I thought people here were so extravagant," she continued. "I have to pay as I go. If I can't pay, then it won't be mine. When I'm going to buy a dress, I might think, 'That's awfully expensive for the fabric that's in it.' Then I have to think if it goes with my wardrobe, will I have to buy shoes or a purse to go with it. Then maybe I'll go back and buy it 24 hours later. Mel thought this was strange. 'If you want it, buy it,' he'd say."

During the tough economic times of the 1980s, Melvin tried other investments, such as radio. Seminole had an FM radio station, along with KSLE, the AM station that serves Seminole, Wewoka, and the surrounding areas. The FM station was a Christian music station and it was for sale. Melvin's good friend, Fred Gipson, suggested finding 10 civic-minded people and each purchasing 10 percent of the station. They wanted to turn the station into one which would boost the community, advertise community events, and help economic development.

"Well, that sounded like a great idea to me," Melvin continued. "And I helped Fred find those 10 people. Of course, I was one of the 10."

The station lost money every month. On a good month, Melvin said, the investors "only lost a little." Melvin's friends, whom he had talked into this "great idea, great investment," could not afford the monthly losses. One by one, either they gave Melvin their interest or he purchased their interest. Melvin ended up with 80 percent. At the end the remaining 20 percent was owned by his neighbor and friend, Charles Johnston.

"Eventually we were able to sell the station for just a fraction of our investment, but it was indeed a very happy day," Melvin said. "This experience taught me a lesson I shall never forget. Do not invest in anything about which you know nothing."

Melvin has served as a director for First National Bank since the late 1960s and that investment seemed to be going pretty well. As a result, when Gene Rainbolt purchased the bank in 1977, Melvin stayed on board.

"First National had been a well-run bank, but Gene's culture took banking to a new level," Melvin said. "I used to refer to Gene as a 'banking genius.'"

Rainbolt bought more banks and, in 1985, placed them in an entity he called United Community Corp. He offered Melvin an opportunity to buy stock in the new corporation. In 1989, United Community Corp became BancFirst.

"My decision to purchase United Community stock in 1985 was the single-best financial decision I have ever made," Melvin said.

Sometimes he thought of the time he turned down a chance to serve on the board of First Federal Savings and Loan.

"If I had been a board member of First Federal Savings and Loan, I would not have been invited to become a director of First National Bank," Melvin said. "Several years later, savings and loan companies throughout the country had a financial crisis. First Federal was one of many who went broke and out of business. All my life I believed that someone up there has been looking out for me. That was certainly true in this instance."

Rainbolt remembers some difficult times in the 1980s.

"The oil industry and some banks were collapsing," Rainbolt said. "But Melvin always stayed calm, made prudent decisions, took no excessive risks. His business ethics make it so easy to deal with him. He's so dependable; you can accept his representations completely. He bends over backwards to be fair. He is insightful as a bank director."

It was to this unstable economic atmosphere that Melvin brought his new idea — a children's museum.

In August of 1988, Melvin and Jasmine took daughter Marilyn and her two daughters to an island in northern Michigan. One day they found themselves with time on their hands.

Not a man to waste time, Melvin went to the tourist center and found a brochure on a Flint, Michigan, children's museum. Following his visit, he was so excited he returned to the motel for a camera to videotape the museum.

The Flint museum was made up of 11,000 square feet in the basement of a bank. Melvin saw it as a place for children to learn and grow.

"We thought, 'We can do this in Seminole,'" Melvin said. And the wheels began to roll.

"Conventional wisdom would say a world-class children's museum couldn't possibly be built in a town of 7,000 with a physical distance of an hour to the closest major metropolitan population," said his daughter, Marilyn. "Who will visit? Who will serve as volunteers? What schools will schedule field trips to such a rural destination? And what foundation would financially support such a tiny place? The answer in most cases would probably be 'no one.'"

Jasmine said both she and Melvin felt Seminole needed the museum.

"It would be a joy to the local children," she said. "We were both concerned about the latchkey children, stuck in front of the television while their parents were both working.

We wanted it to be more than for the children in Seminole. We thought, if we're not going to do this, there is no point in having wealth. We've had wealthy friends who did wonderful things with their money and they were quiet with it. I always wondered why people have private jets, their own hotel rooms; we always travel coach. If you don't do good with money, then I don't know why God gave it to you.

"I tell Melvin that he made a lot of money taking something from the ground and that if you put nothing back, you have raped the earth," Jasmine said. "You can only wear so many shoes, so many pairs of pants. A life like that would drive me nuts. I didn't come from it and I wouldn't want it. Besides that, my mother would stand up in her grave and say, 'If you can't do better than that, you should just leave.'"

Melvin's plan involved inviting 15 people, mostly mothers and educators, who he thought might be excited and helpful to lunch at the Gusher Inn.

Marci Donaho, a teacher at Northwood Elementary, was one of those on the list. "I wasn't going to go, but then I saw they had beanie weenies in the school cafeteria that day, so I did," she joked.

It was March 15, 1989. Melvin showed them his video and those gathered agreed — "Let's do it."

"I remember thinking, 'What am I doing here?'" Donaho said. "They asked me to do something and I said yes, but I didn't even know what they wanted from me. People can't say no to Melvin. I guess it's because of his demeanor. His size is part of his charm, as well as his smile."

Melvin believes Donaho, who later became the museum's

executive director, is a major reason for the museum's success.

"I cannot imagine the museum without her leadership," he said. "She has been an integral part of every fundraising presentation. Her passion and her love for children sell the museum. Jasmine and I are known as the museum's co-founders. Marci should also be named as a co-founder. From the very beginning, she has been either the board president or the executive director. Her fingerprints are on every inch of the museum."

Gene Rainbolt, Melvin's banking partner, said everyone Melvin knew was asked to be part of the museum.

"I was the original skeptic," Rainbolt said. "Nobody but Melvin could have succeeded in that project. I wouldn't have had the nerve to take it on."

"When he came to talk to me about the museum, in my mind I was saying, 'This is never going to work; there is no way this can work,'" said Robert Henry. "But I can't tell Melvin that. I can't not help him, even thought I know we will both go down in flames.

"I don't think I have ever been so wrong. I was feeling bad about my lack of faith on this until four or five of the others said they felt the same way," Henry continued. "They didn't think it would succeed either, but we love Melvin Moran and couldn't tell him no. We were prepared to go off the cliff with him. He's just a visionary."

Henry, like every other person Melvin asked, made every call he was asked to make, talked to everybody he was supposed to, and did everything he could to help Melvin make his dream come true. Many believe the museum is Melvin and Jasmine Moran's greatest accomplishment.

"We decided that if ours was to be a success, it had to be extra special to attract families from long distances," Melvin said. "We decided to make it the best one in the country."

They bought the Power Transmission building in Seminole, along with seven and one-half acres. This firm, which had built a beautiful new building, had gone bankrupt. Marilyn's video company made a video. An architect made them a scale model and Melvin hit the fundraising circuit.

Melvin's original plan was to compose a letter and send it to 200 people but a professional fundraiser told him he would be lucky to raise enough money to pay for his stamps with that plan. "She said you have to go to people you know," Melvin said. "I've been on a lot of boards, so I'm able to open doors."

He first approached Kerr-McGee Corporation, where he was told they already had expended their giving budget for that year.

"But Kerr-McGee Vice President Tom McDaniel looked at the video I brought and then said, 'Tell us how Kerr-McGee can help you,'" Melvin said. "They generously gave the project $10,000, which was our first corporate donation."

With the Kerr-McGee name in their pocket, other doors opened.

"The average time it takes to open a museum like this is five years," Melvin said. "Ours opened in four years and three months."

It would have been easier to hire experienced talent to build and grow the museum, but that was not Melvin Moran's way. "Instead, this hands-on angel has nurtured, guided, supported ,and loved this very special place every single day," Marilyn said.

The Jasmine Moran Children's Museum opened to the public on January 23, 1993.

"At first I was concerned when Mel gave the museum my name," Jasmine said. "I would have preferred that it be called the Moran Museum."

But once again Melvin's personal friendship with God directed the order of his life.

"We were in Colorado and I began having a problem," Jasmine said. "With the altitude, my blood pressure began dropping and wouldn't respond to medication. I was hospitalized. I became very ill and the doctor said, 'I'm losing her and I don't know why. I've done everything I can to stop the blood pressure from dropping.'"

"He said the only thing that might help was prayer. I'm a firm believer in prayer," Melvin said.

"They had a little chapel in the hospital and Melvin went in and prayed," Jasmine said. "When he came back, the doctor said, 'A miracle has taken place. Her blood pressure has stopped dropping. I don't know if it was your prayer or our hope.'"

Jasmine stayed awhile longer in Colorado with their daughter and Melvin flew home.

"It was then that he announced that the museum would be named after me," Jasmine said. "I was aggravated at the time. I told him, 'Melvin, you might as well not have prayed. They only name things after people when they're dead. Now you've done it.'"

People visiting the museum will often look at the plaque with Jasmine's name on it, engraved with her birthdate, and say, "When did she die?"

"But I've teased him about that long enough, I guess,"

Jasmine said, laughing.

Of the 24 well-known people in Oklahoma that Melvin asked to serve on an advisory board, 22 said yes. Their name recognition, like his, smoothed the way many times.

"The majority became active, doing fundraisers like celebrity golf tournaments," Melvin said. "Most are donors as well. As for the original Seminole board members, we later decided the board should reflect a state focus. Now there are 90 or 95 members from all over Oklahoma, all creative people. When you ask for a grant, it's helpful to see that these people believe in our project."

Donaho served as board president until June, 1996, when she was hired as executive director.

"I had to leave school," she said, and still gets a little teary when she thinks of all the children she had taught and the ones for whom she would not be there. But at the museum, her opportunity to reach children is unparalleled.

"I felt safe because we had this group of well-respected people who said we could do this," she said. "We had a committed support system. At no point did any of us say we can't do this. There was no tone of doubt."

But it was harder to leave the classroom than Donaho thought.

"I was clearing out my desk," she said, sitting in her office at the museum. "I remember worrying if I was making the right decision. In the empty classroom, I saw the faces of the kids who had blessed my life. I knew nothing about running a business, which a museum is. I knew it was a chance to do something special for kids. I spotted the Bible on my desk and turned to Ecclesiastes: 'to everything there is s season.' I still miss the classroom to this day. Every retired teacher will tell you the same thing. But today there was an anonymous letter praising our work here at the museum. It was like sunshine radiating from my soul."

The museum has expanded six times to nearly 40,000 square feet and 22 acres. It recently recorded 60,000 annual visitors. It has won many awards, including the 2007 Outstanding Attraction Award at the Governor's Conference on Tourism.

"The reason the Children's Museum has won national and international acclaim is because that nurturing, guidance, support and love [that Melvin gives] is a magnet for children who know it when they see it," said Marilyn. "Dad's love for kids is very real and very alive in this amazing place."

Melvin, at 78, visits the museum every single day.

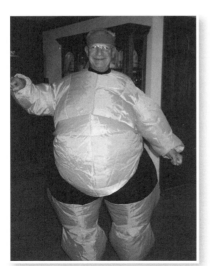

"He goes out on the floor, reads the guest book, visits with people," Donaho said. "He asks where they're from and how they found out about the museum."

At age 72, Melvin, still the comedy entertainer, dressed up as a sumo wrestler for the Jasmine Moran Children's Museum's Great Pumpkin Event in 2002.

His schedule has him at the museum mid- to late-morning, when he has tea with his long-time friend Cecil Sullivan at Lunch 'n' Such.

"But always before lunch," Donaho said.

Because Melvin spends time at the museum every day, Donaho and he have developed a very close professional and social friendship.

"I can joke with Melvin, tell him things I can't tell anyone else," she said. "Sometimes we agree to disagree. If he doesn't get his way, he'll say, 'Marci, I'll have to trust your judgment,' but he'll go to the nth degree to change my mind. If he still doesn't get his way, he's a gentleman and accepts it. But that doesn't happen often. He doesn't allow himself to go to a negative place. If he feels strongly about something, he'll trudge on to get his way. And he's usually right. It's never 'all about me,' but all about what's best."

Donaho said she's only seen Melvin angry one time. He never uses obscenities, but once when he was angry at a sheriff, Melvin called him a scoundrel.

Is Melvin her boss? Donaho said she has 15 bosses — the museum's executive board. "The person in this office has to run the museum. Though most people think so, I don't consider Melvin my boss," she said. "I consider him the deputy museum director. He just gives me ideas and trusts my judgment."

Donaho told the museum board in 2007 that she would retire in two years. "I wanted them to think about getting someone in to shadow me for six months or a year," she said. "But by the end of the day: I was just sick," she said. "I can't retire from this place. I can't sit at home and watch the good stuff going on here without me."

She talked to her husband, Dale, who recommended going to Melvin about how she felt and, after about two weeks, she did.

"That's the best news I've ever heard," Melvin told her.

Both she and Melvin worry about the museum's future when both of them are no longer around to nurture it.

"Right now we're THE children's museum of Oklahoma," Donaho said. "I worry about when we no longer have the physical presence of Melvin Moran around to open doors. I'm 60; if God gives me 20 more years, I'll still be here.

"But it will be a challenge to find someone new with this passion," she continued. "You can't train it. I don't know anyone else who has it, besides Dale. You can't expect others to have it just because we do. Dale's seen it through our eyes, but there aren't many others. The next person will see it as a business and that's not bad, but it could change the culture. The next person won't feel all corny and mushy about this like we do."

To that end, the museum's board has been working hard to build a foundation nest egg that will fund the museum's operation into perpetuity.

The most recent expansion is a joint project among five of Oklahoma's major healthcare providers. Kim Henry, First Lady of Oklahoma, was instrumental in bringing all the participants of the $500,000 project together.

"Well, that wasn't my puzzle," she said when asked about her input. "I just put two pieces together."

Melvin said Mrs. Henry asked to be given something to do for the museum and he mentioned the renovation of the hospital wing.

"I asked him how much it would cost and he said about $100,000," Mrs. Henry said.

The Morans were close friends with Governor and Mrs. Brad Henry even before Henry was elected governor.

First Lady Kim Henry chatted with Melvin and his son-in-law Gary Kleiman during a museum event in early 2007.

She asked him if he knew a certain Integris official and, because Melvin did not, Mrs. Henry offered to speak to him on behalf of the museum. When he heard their presentation, he asked to see the museum.

"When he left, I told Melvin, 'We got it!'" Mrs. Henry said. Sure enough when the Integris [Baptist Medical Center] official visited the museum, Mrs. Henry said his remarks were, "I don't think you're thinking big enough."

"I have never heard anybody tell Melvin Moran he doesn't think big enough!" Mrs. Henry said, laughing. Integris not only gave $100,000, but helped contact four other hospitals for $100,000 each. Mrs. Henry gave a dinner for the donors at the Governor's Mansion to seal the deal.

"I remember the first time I met Melvin Moran," Mrs. Henry said. The Henrys had been close to the Moran family for a long time.

"My father-in-law had such tremendous respect for Melvin," she said. Mrs. Henry met Melvin at the first dinner for the museum.

"Melvin was just as delightful as my father-in-law said he was," she said. "There were a lot of people there who gave a lot of money to help the museum get started.

"Brad [Governor Brad Henry] and I were just married, still young. He was in law school and we didn't have any money to give to the museum. But you wouldn't have known that by the way Melvin treated us. He treated everyone the same, large donor or not. It's an incredible characteristic.

"When we left, I turned to Brad and said, 'Did your father give him a lot of money in our name?' and he said 'no.' I was amazed. Melvin was just so warm. He makes everyone feel at home. Melvin has such passion, such integrity and character, and because of that everyone got on board. You just want to help him. His enthusiasm is infectious. He's definitely a rare individual."

Similarly, the governor's cousin, Robert Henry, helped out with a donation to the museum. "I didn't have the kind of money some people have, but I had some I wanted to give," he said. "Melvin said, 'Here's what we have a need for: give this money instead to create a little scholarship fund to pay the small entrance fee that we'll have for kids who can't afford it at all.' That was a great idea. The next time he was talking about the museum to a group, he said, 'Attorney General Henry established this scholarship,' giving all the credit to me for the modest contribution I made. That's Melvin Moran for you."

Mrs. Henry cites the museum's success as proof of Melvin's enthusiasm and ability to inspire others to do good works. "The museum inspires creativity and imagination," she said. "Children go into the museum and see opportunity and learn work ethics. They play in the grocery store; they crawl into the airplane cockpit, it inspires a lifelong love. They get so caught up in imagination they don't realize how much they're learning.

"And if we fire creativity and imagination, it teaches children divergent thinking. I do think you can teach creativity — oh, not to be a Da Vinci or a Mozart — but you can teach creative thought, thinking outside the box, analytical thinking. And that makes kids more successful in education and in life."

Whenever Jasmine and Melvin travel to another city, they make a point to visit the children's museum if there is one.

Recently while in Honolulu, Hawaii, they had the hotel desk clerk call to make sure the museum was open because of a rain storm that had just passed through. The clerk gave their names to the museum receptionist and the Morans took a taxi to the museum.

"When we arrived, I pulled out my billfold to pay and the woman at the desk said, 'No, we won't take your money,'" Melvin said. "Before I had a chance to question this strange statement, another woman arrived at the desk holding up about 15 photographs. The top picture was of her and me. To say the least, I was absolutely amazed. The remainder of the photographs had been taken of exhibits at the Jasmine Moran Children's Museum."

Apparently the woman, president of the board of directors, and her daughter, the museum's executive director, were in St. Louis, Missouri, for a convention and decided to take the seven-hour side trip to Seminole to visit the Children's Museum.

"I happened to be at the museum and gave them a tour," Melvin said. "I must admit that I did not remember any of that. But there were the pictures to prove it."

Museum-Quality Friendships

"I can't believe he stayed. He could have gone any-place. He has kept this town alive. And this project reflects his love of this place."

— Donna Terry

The museum provided an opportunity for Melvin to stay in touch with some of his oldest friends. One of those was Donna Pollock Terry, who had moved to California in eighth grade and worked as a fashion illustrator in advertising for the last 40 years. Her work was featured in many newspapers and stores throughout San Francisco and the Bay area. During those years, she had lost touch with Melvin and their old elementary school friend from Seminole, Joe Snider.

"When I was in my 60s, I was cleaning out an old address book and found Joe's number," Terry said. "I decided to try it to make sure it no longer worked before I tossed it out. He was a big shot lawyer in Oklahoma City by then and the number was for his home."

When Terry called, Joe Snider answered the phone. As they renewed their friendship, Joe invited the Terrys to Oklahoma. About a year later, they came.

"Most of the times that we came, we stayed in Oklahoma City with Joe, but once he said, 'How about driving to Seminole to see the old home place,'" Terry said. "He told me that Melvin was still there, and in fact, had been the mayor. So we went.

"And it was astounding to me! Every other kid had left. There weren't that many opportunities in Seminole. The town had gone downhill after the oil boom. Melvin and his family were very, very bright people with a lot of strength and the ability to go wherever they wanted. That they stayed in Seminole, where there were no Jews that I knew of, was amazing. That he'd married this beautiful showgirl and brought her here…well, we had a very sophisticated way of life in San Francisco, so I could imagine what this lovely woman gave up in coming here."

Terry does not remember what she expected of Melvin's showgirl wife, but found her to be warm and friendly.

"We became very good friends," Terry said. "She told me about coming to live here, about the heat and hanging her wash outside. Sometimes it would blow away. She and I both have this very delicate skin and she'd get sunburned. I cannot imagine it. I love Oklahoma, but not the storms and the heat. Well, of course I'm sitting on an earthquake fault here in San Francisco."

Melvin, Terry said, was "the same old Melvin."

"He even still had a tiny lisp," she said.

Joe Snider had filled her in on the museum project and Melvin, of course, wanted to take them to see it.

"Melvin had this great big car we could all fit in and he drove us all around and helped us catch up," Terry said. "He showed us where we used to live and we were shocked. It used to be the best part of town. He took us to the cemetery. I had people buried there and he helped me find them. I cried because all those people I'd known and grown up with were gone. Melvin and Jasmine were so good to put up with my emotions out there. So sweet and charming."

When she saw the new museum, it was a large empty warehouse.

"Melvin told us about his dream," Terry said. "At no time did he ever say anything about money. He had his first exhibit, a robot, but it wasn't working yet. The more Melvin and Jasmine talked about the dream, the more I thought, 'I can't believe he stayed. He could have gone anyplace. He has kept this town alive. And this project reflects his love of this place.'"

As the group was leaving, Donna and her husband, Ivan Terry, trailed behind.

"My husband said, 'Let's put something towards this project,'" she said. "So we wrote a check and gave it to Melvin and he was so surprised. I think he was also proud that we believed in the project, too. I remember that he said, 'God bless you.' I've heard a thousand people say those words, but I still cry when I think of the way he said it."

Being part of the museum kept the Terrys close to the Morans. They asked Joe Snider to keep them updated on it and when they later saw how beautiful the museum was, they decided to leave their estate to it.

"We don't have any children or family to leave it to and we were going to leave it to the Oakland Zoo because they didn't have a house big enough for the elephant," Terry said. "But later we decided the city would take care of the animals…

they have since built a bigger house for the elephant. So we redid our will and left it to the museum."

A couple of years later Melvin asked the couple back to Seminole for a banquet he was giving for the donors.

"It was a big affair with Senator Boren and a federal judge, to thank all the donors for what they'd done," Terry said. "Now here's the thing about Oklahomans and it's such a radical contrast from our environment — Oklahomans love each other. They take care of each other. They honor each other."

At the banquet Judge Robert Henry began making the announcement of the donor of the year.

"He described this couple who had left everything to the museum and we realized he was talking about us," Terry said. "He brought out a big plaque and invited us up to the podium.

"I was dumb-founded, speechless," she said. "Well, I tried to make a speech, but I screwed it all up and I've spent the rest of my life wishing I could have said what I would have said, if I'd had time to prepare.

"I would have said, 'When we were children in Seminole, we had nothing like this museum. We had the movie theater, stamp collecting, and play. How much our lives would have been enriched if we had known what was out there for us. Now the children of Oklahoma have the Jasmine Moran Children's Museum. How much more will their lives be because of it?"

To Terry, "Melvin's dream" is not like most children's museums.

"This one isn't a play place," she said. "It's a place where children can experience being a doctor or a lawyer or whatever, so they can be a part of what the world will be. In the medical part, they walk on crutches, see what it's like to be blind, or live your life in a wheelchair. When we were kids, we made fun of people in wheel chairs! The museum teaches them to respect one another. A child learns while playing and that's why it was so inspiring to us."

The Terrys bought a brick for the brick street for everyone they knew.

"We honored our friends, our doctors, people who would never come here or know that we'd honored them," Terry said. "I think it's beautiful that the bricks are the color of the Oklahoma soil."

Since their reunion, the Terrys and the Morans have become close and frequently vacation together.

"I remember one time Melvin said it was our turn to choose a vacation," Terry said. "He could never be gone for more than a week. So I chose a trip up Puget Sound on a wooden sailing vessel. Jasmine had just had a knee surgery and I wasn't aware of what she'd gone through. We got to the boat and we had to climb up a ladder and over into the ship. It was then that I realized that she was in a lot of pain. I had no idea how she was going to get her knee over into the boat. But she did."

The couples were shocked by the conditions of the boat. They had always been private people and, in these conditions, the Morans and the Terrys were basically bunking together. Only a little petition screened their dressing.

"Apparently Melvin snores — loudly," Terry continued. "We were all sleeping within 20 feet of each other. My husband

and Melvin were sleeping in the farthest part of the cabin, my husband about an arm's length away from Melvin. He can sleep through anything, but he tells the story of one night being awakened by a white apparition feeling its way across the cabin. It was Jasmine in her nightgown and she made her way over to Melvin, shook him to make him quit snoring, and then floated away — she never said a word.

"By the end of the vacation, we all felt like we knew each other very well!"

Melvin's snoring is somewhat of a legend in the Moran family. In about 1990, Jasmine picked up a catalog and noticed a gadget guaranteed to stop snoring. She asked Melvin if he would try it and he agreed.

Six weeks later the gadget arrived, a bracelet connected to a wire, which was connected to a heavy duty battery and a miniature microphone with a clip. The snorer was supposed to clip on the microphone and put on the bracelet. When he or she snored, the microphone picked up the sound and sent an electric charge to the bracelet to wake up the snorer.

"So that evening I hooked myself up," Melvin said. "And I gotta' tell you, it works. I didn't snore once during that entire night. I was afraid to shut my eyes! But the downside of it was that on this particular night, Jasmine snored. And every time she snored, I got shocked. We have a small dog that sleeps in our bed. When the newspaper was delivered at 5:00 a.m., our dog barked and I got shocked again. At 7:00 a.m., the phone rang and I was darn near electrocuted!"

Melvin's inability to relax while on vacation is well known

to anyone who has traveled with the Morans. It figured prominently in the Alaskan vacation that David once planned for his parents.

"I try to be as much like my father as possible," David said. "Personality-wise and as a public speaker, I think I am very like him. But one way I am not like him is that I enjoy leisure time more than he does.

"When I was in law school, my wife Kris and I spent a summer in Alaska where I was doing a legal internship," David said. "Mom and Dad decided to take a cruise and end up in Juneau where we were. I was trying to think of something to do with them and planned a few days in Tenakee Springs, about 50 miles west of Juneau."

The only way to get to Tenakee Springs is by ferry or float plane. There is one inn with four rooms and a restaurant with one table. There is no television or other entertainment, except for the hot springs. There is a bathhouse to soak in the springs. Visitors walk in beautiful woods or hang out in the harbor watching whales.

"This was heaven for us, but torture for him," David said. "He'd never been away from the telephone before. At one point we were walking along the one road and Dad burst into a trot – he thought he'd seen a phone booth. He was so disappointed when it wasn't.

"He was a good sport and pretended to have a good time, but he told me a few months later that he had a nightmare after he got back. He went to a doctor and was told there was something wrong with his heart. The doctor was sending him to

Tenakee Springs!"

The most recent trip Melvin and Jasmine took to their beloved Israel was with Donna and Ivan Terry.

"That was an eye-opener," Mrs. Terry said. "Melvin invited us to go. They'd been many times, and to go with Jews who know the country made the trip very special."

Because Melvin's family has contributed heavily to Israel, the president of the travel company was their guide. Each day, he enriched their trip with special things because of Melvin. The Terrys enjoyed many things that Melvin and Jasmine had seen and done before, but they were happy to share it all again with their friends, things like floating in the Dead Sea and taking mud baths.

"My husband and I are agnostic, which doesn't mean that we don't believe, only that we don't know," Terry said. "It took years of searching for us to come to this. Melvin had the guide show us both sides of Israel, the Christian and Jewish parts, and there were plenty of places Melvin wouldn't have gone if it weren't for us. It was so much more meaningful to us that way.

"The guide had planned our visit to Jerusalem for last. He set it up so we came to the old highway, rounded a mountain, and saw it all laid out in front of us. It was a gray day. He brought out some wine and told us about this ceremony where you share wine when you come to Jerusalem."

The guide began singing "Jerusalem of Gold" in Hebrew. And from the back of the bus, Jasmine began singing it with him, but in English.

"She has a most exquisite voice," Terry said. "It was like

they'd practiced; it was so beautiful. Then they switched and both sang it in English. What a way to be introduced to Jerusalem! And there were so many other things that they opened up for us. We had the red carpet treatment the whole week. We paid our own way, so I know it wasn't that they'd paid extra for all that. It was just because of Melvin."

The foursome also visited Melvin's family, which still lives in Israel.

"Melvin has about 30 relatives still in Israel and he held a big banquet for them," Terry said. "He had brought gifts for each one. They love him."

From Jerusalem, the Terrys were going on to Jordan.

"I think it's dangerous for Jews to go into a Muslim country, especially someone as important as Melvin," Terry said. "There is always someone being killed, something being blown up. In fact, there had been a shooting at the spot where the guide was supposed to meet us.

"Just before we were to meet the guide, we were at the Wailing Wall. It was so unusual to see people praying to a wall, but it gives you the same devout feeling they have. You could wrap up a message and put it in the wall, like a prayer. There were thousands of them in the wall.

"It was kind of emotional when we were leaving Melvin and Jasmine. They were going home and we were going into what could be a dangerous situation. I remember Melvin whispering in my ear that he had put a prayer in the wall that we'd be safe in Jordan. Of all the people he could have said a prayer for..."

During that trip to Israel, Melvin told the Terrys about his conversation with God, which had taken place during his previous trip to Jerusalem. It was only the second time he had told the story. Jasmine was the first to hear it.

"We're always feeling Melvin's presence, like a spiritual thing," Terry said. "We believe in him. If anybody could have been touched by God, it's Melvin."

Now, years after changing their will to leave their estate to the Children's Museum, Terry says there will not be as much as she had once hoped.

"Now we've spent nearly all our money and there won't be much for the museum when we're gone," she said. "But Melvin is still appreciative. It's a beautiful feeling, unfaltering friendship. We say 'I love you' so easily. We always know they are there for us. Even Melvin and Jasmine don't realize all the ways they've touched our lives."

"Every few months, Donna and Ivan have made generous donations to the museum," Melvin said. "I have been very moved by their generosity. They are wonderful and generous friends."

Of Humor and Humility

"To watch him… make these gifts no one else ever knew about…he didn't make them feel beholden. You'd think he was the one getting the gift! He'd thank them for letting him be their friend, for what they did in the community."

— David Boren

Through Melvin's life, the recurring threads are humor and humility.

He and Jasmine have been instrumental in bringing Christmas dinner to Seminole's needy for more than 25 years, patterning it after Oklahoma City's Red Andrews Christmas dinner. Many people have said the dinner is really Melvin's way of taking care of his community.

"The Rotary sponsors the dinner, actually a luncheon, on Christmas Day," he said. "It was designed to provide food, friendship, and good company for the needy, elderly, and lonely."

"He has such compassion, such an incredibly generous heart," said his friend, David Boren. "One of the things I always enjoyed was participating in the community Christmas dinner. I wonder how many people knew that Melvin was the driving force behind that. How unusual that a person of the Jewish faith would be the leader of the Christmas celebration. But it wouldn't have happened without him. He just kept on every single year."

Many may not be aware that, in addition to working with Rotary on the dinner, Melvin privately has a long list of people he just happens to know about who needs extra food during the holidays, clothing for children, and the bare necessities. He has a habit around the Christmas season of buying enormous amounts of food and clothing for 25 or so families. He would take these things to their homes himself. It might take a couple of days, because there were so many people to deliver to.

"He allowed me to go with him a couple of times," Boren said. "We went, just the two of us. To watch him do these things, make these gifts no one else ever knew about…the way he treated the people. He didn't make them feel beholden, not like they were taking a handout. You'd think he was the one getting the gift! He went like a guest into their homes, not as someone giving charity," Boren marveled. "The things he'd say made them feel so good, made them feel like the special people they were. He'd thank them for letting him be their friend, for what they did in the community. It was amazing to see him help them meet their physical needs and feel good about themselves.

"He'd go back and bring them things they needed at other times of the year as well, keeping a watch on them, treating everyone in the community like a member of his own family," Boren said. "It's the greatest gift anyone can give someone else."

In 2005, the local paper printed an advance story on the dinner, quoting an elderly woman saying, "I think Melvin Moran is the nicest person in the whole world." During the dinner, an elderly woman came over to Melvin and identified herself as the woman who was quoted in the paper. When Melvin thanked her, she apologized for her remark. "I got mixed up," she said. "I wasn't talking about you. I was talking about Don Gill [another who helps with the dinner]."

Melvin has been mistaken for another on at least one other occasion. One day in the grocery store a man Melvin did not recognize approached him and said, "I just want to say thank you for taking care of me when I broke my leg." Melvin thought the man might have been hurt while working heavy equipment for Moran Pipe and Supply and so he just said, "I'm so glad you have recovered." As the man walked away, he said, "Goodbye, Dr. Davis."

Recently Jasmine asked him to take back an item she bought at Sharpe's Department Store, located on Main Street in Seminole. Sharpe's previously had been located on the west side of the street, now home to the Salvation Army, but had moved to the east side of the street many years ago.

"I hadn't noticed that they'd moved," Melvin said. "So I went into the Salvation Army store, found a sales clerk and said to her, 'My wife was shopping here yesterday, purchased this shirt and she got the wrong size. I need to exchange the shirt.'"

The response was, "Mr. Moran, I don't believe your wife shops here."

"Then I realized where I was," Melvin said.

Although a stickler for detail in his professional life, Melvin's reputation of being oblivious to his surroundings and a little unclear about the normal workings of day-to-day life are legendary — as is the Morans' love of animals.

"Their house is a veritable animalerie," said Robert Henry, choosing the French word for "house of animals." "You never know what critter in what various state of recuperation will be housed there at Chez Moran."

Melvin says that Jasmine is knowledgeable about animals but he is not. He uses as an example of the black chow who showed up one day and adopted them.

"We were a little leery at first because we had heard that chows can be pretty mean," Melvin said. "But our chow was loveable, we thought. We named her Sheba."

One evening while Melvin was downstairs, he heard a terrible barking and growling from the backyard. Opening the backdoor, he found Sheba had killed a possum.

"So what to do?" he thought. "I did the only thing I could think of. I took a large paper bag outdoors. I have some large pincers. I picked up the possum with the pincers, put it in the paper bag, and put it in our polycart where we put our garbage."

Later Jasmine, who had not heard the commotion, came downstairs and Melvin told her about the incident.

"Was the possum all bloody?" she asked.

"No, it wasn't," Melvin said.

"Did you see any blood at all?" she asked.

"No, I don't think I did," Melvin said.

"Then how do you know it was dead?" Jasmine questioned.

"Well, I just assumed," Melvin said.

"I think you had better go and take the possum out of the

polycart," she said.

"So I gingerly took the sack out of the polycart and watched as the possum walked away," Melvin said.

For all his endearing naiveté, Melvin is extremely intelligent and well organized. He is recognized for his time management skills and has conducted numerous seminars to help others learn the art.

He keeps himself organized with the use of calendars at home and in his office, and by carrying a piece of paper in his pocket listing what he expects to accomplish that day. He's done this for more than 50 years.

"From time to time, one of the students at a time management seminar will say, 'You have changed my life,'" Melvin said.

Even so, there are times when Melvin sometimes gets a little confused.

"I am, I think, a well-organized person," he said. "There are usually 15 or 20 items on that list, in the order I hope to accomplish these tasks. I refer to this sheet as my memo sheet. While I am well organized, I am probably the least observant person on the planet. It is not uncommon for me to notice something in my office, such as a picture hanging on the wall, and asking how long it's been there. The response, more often than not, is 'Years.'"

Every Thursday afternoon for decades, Jasmine has had her hair done at the hairdressers. Because Melvin is not an observant person, he seldom noticed that her hair had been done and therefore seldom commented on it. Jasmine was a little hurt by his lack of attention. So Melvin decided the best way to rectify the situation was to write "Compliment Jasmine on her hair" on his list every Thursday.

"And it worked beautifully," Melvin said. "Jasmine felt good about being noticed and I felt good about remembering."

Melvin's system worked for two years until Jasmine went to the dentist instead of the hairdresser on a particular Thursday. When Melvin arrived home after work, and on cue from his memo sheet, said, "Jasmine, your hair looks lovely," he was informed that her hair was "a mess."

"I no longer use my memo sheet to remind me of Jasmine's hairdresser day," Melvin said. "I simply wing it; I seldom get it right."

Another who knows first-hand about the power of "the list" is Robert Henry.

When Henry decided to apply for the position of 10th Circuit Court of Appeals judge, he asked Melvin to broach the subject of a recommendation from David Boren. Melvin brought out the "list," wrote himself a note and the next day he came back to Henry with Boren's comments.

"Here's this guy operating way up there on a high intellectual level, but he has so many balls in the air, he has developed this defense mechanism," Henry said. "The list is omnipresent. Once at a restaurant, he left the list on the table. He rushed back and, to his dismay, they had cleaned the table off and thrown away the list. He went through the garbage to find his list.

"Who knows what good deeds would not have gotten done that day if Melvin hadn't found his grease-stained, food-stained hand-written list in the trash," Henry said.

Even the "omnipresent" list does not help sometimes as Melvin goes through his life always tightly focused on the task at hand. There was one time he was so focused he did not even notice his wife on the side of the road.

Jasmine's stepfather, Michael Geselle, who lived in Canada before his death, came to visit while Melvin was still working at Moran Pipe and Supply on West Broadway, about a mile from downtown Seminole.

On that day, Jasmine and her stepfather were shopping downtown. They planned that Melvin would pick them up at a certain spot on his way home. But, arriving a little early, Geselle suggested walking on toward Melvin's office. Jasmine worried that Melvin might not see them if they did.

"Mike was wearing a very large and very loud Hawaiian shirt," Jamine said. "Mike said, 'That's impossible. There's no way that Melvin could drive by us without seeing us.'"

As they walked toward Melvin's office, at least a dozen cars stopped and offered them a ride; they politely told everyone that Melvin would be along shortly.

"Of course, I drove right by them, even though they were frantically waving and yelling at me," Melvin said. "And because they were not in the appointed spot, I went on home, leaving them temporarily stranded!"

In 1990, Jasmine and Melvin attended an oil convention in Reno, Nevada. While the group had reservations, all the group rate rooms had been assigned when the Morans arrived. They were upgraded to a room with a raised round bed with a mirrored ceiling and floor-to-ceiling red velvet drapes.

"We could never figure out which end of the bed was the head or the foot," Melvin said. "Since the bed was raised off the floor about a foot, every time I got out of bed, I fell to the floor."

Another oil convention in San Francisco, California, was held at the "very fancy" Mark Hopkins Hotel. As they checked in, the registration clerk could not find the Morans' name. When Melvin told him that the reservation was made several months ago, he looked again, but still could not find it. He asked if Melvin possibly could have made the reservation through the oil association rather than directly through the hotel. He tried to call the oil association, but it was closed.

"The room clerk was very apologetic," Melvin said. "He said he was sorry, but he couldn't find my name and the hotel was completely full. He further said that every hotel in downtown San Francisco was full. I don't become indignant very often, but I did that day. I reiterated that this reservation was made months ago and they absolutely had to find a room for me."

The clerk assigned the Morans an entire ballroom.

"It was huge," Melvin said. "There were several bars in the room. There was not a bed, so they brought one in. They also brought in a clothing rack. So Jasmine and I spent our several convention days in this huge ballroom.

"And when we got back to Seminole, I saw on my desk the hotel reservation form. I had forgotten to send it in."

Melvin has, on several occasions, been asked to introduce the governor, most recently as the representative of Oklahoma's Higher Education Alumni Council (HEACO), an organization of college officials.

One day of the year is designated as Higher Education Day, with representatives from all the colleges meeting at the Capitol, visiting their senators and representatives, and then meeting in the House of Representatives for speeches about higher education.

A few years ago, Melvin was asked to make one of those speeches and, as usual for Melvin, he inserted a little levity.

"That may have been the reason I was invited back," he joked.

On the second visit, he was invited to introduce Governor Brad Henry, which Melvin considered quite an honor.

Among Melvin's many awards and accomplishments is the 2006 Higher Education Alumni Council of Oklahoma (HEACO) award, presented by HEACO Chair Carlos Johnson and Seminole State College President Dr. Jim Utterback.

"I meticulously wrote what I thought was a good introduction of the governor, as far as his record on higher education, which was an outstanding record," Melvin said.

There were several speakers and when the master of ceremonies introduced Melvin, the HEACO director whispered to Melvin that she had just heard from the governor and he was running late. He would not arrive for another 12 minutes. He was asked to ad lib.

"I had approximately 10 seconds to prepare a 12-minute speech to college officials, state office holders, and hundreds who supported higher education around the state," Melvin said. "So what to do? Well, I said the only thing I could think of to say. 'You have been sitting her for a very long time listening to speeches about higher education. So I am going to give you a break and tell you some stories that have nothing to do with higher education."

Melvin spent the next several minutes regaling the crowd with the humorous stories of his life. Finally someone told him the governor was there and Melvin was able to give his introduction.

"And the governor came to the microphone and said, 'Melvin that was the nicest introduction I have ever had,'" Melvin said. "I don't know whether he was referring to my real introduction or whether he was referring to my remarks prior to the introduction."

Pieces of History

"He [Dean McGee] did most of the talking, reminiscing about... those boom days when he was a young geologist for the Phillips Petroleum Company..."
— Melvin Moran

Melvin's life has encompassed more than three-quarters of a century and he has lived through many historic events. He has had the opportunity to be part of history several times and has learned first-hand about historic events from those who made history.

"I am fascinated by stories of historical events which are told by persons who actually participated in the events," Melvin said.

One such memorable conversation was a two-hour visit on the history of the oilfield with Dean McGee, co-founder of Kerr-McGee Oil Corporation. McGee was a young geologist for Phillips Petroleum when the Fixico No. 1, discovery well of the Greater Seminole Oilfield, was drilled. The Greater Seminole Field soon became the largest oilfield in the world.

The Fixico No. 1 was drilled east of Seminole in the Wilcox formation in July, 1926. In 1976, to commemorate the 50th anniversary, a huge celebration was planned by the city of Seminole. Among the festivities was a parade featuring bands, floats, and hundreds of trucks with oilfield equipment. That

CHAPTER TWENTY

In 1976, on the 50th anniversary of the drilling of the Fixico No. 1 discovery well for the Greater Seminole Oilfield, a marker was dedicated to commemorate the historic event. The field would later become the largest oilfield in the world. David Boren addresses the crowd with oilfield greats Dean A. McGee, left, and Melvin, second from right, looking on.

evening a banquet was scheduled to feature Governor David Boren and McGee was asked to be the keynote speaker.

Two weeks before the event, McGee's secretary asked the event planners for a briefing at McGee's Oklahoma City office. Because of his busy schedule, the meeting was set for 6:00 a.m. and slated to last only 15 minutes.

The Seminole delegation of five, including Melvin, arrived in the Kerr-McGee building and entered the elevator with a nondescript man that no one would have guessed was the world renowned Dean McGee.

"I think you are coming to see me," McGee said, and

introduced himself to the surprised visitors.

"He ushered us into the Kerr-McGee board room and we sat around this beautiful table," Melvin remembered. "Though we were there to tell him about our event, he did most of the talking, reminiscing about his recollections of those boom days when he was a young geologist for the Phillips Petroleum Company, working out of their Shawnee office."

The 15-minute meeting lasted 90 minutes. Then McGee accompanied the Seminole residents through his outer office to the elevator.

"As we passed through the outer office, we could not help but notice approximately a dozen men waiting patiently to see Mr. McGee," Melvin said. "All were wearing suits and everyone had a briefcase. Their business must have been more important than ours."

As the elevator door was closing, McGee reached through the door, causing the door to reopen. He joined them in the elevator, saying, "I want to show you something."

They got out of the elevator on the concourse level, where a lighted tunnel led them to the parking garage. Along the walls were 20 large paintings, all relating the history of the Kerr-McGee Oil Corporation.

"As we walked through the tunnel, Dean McGee related to us the story behind each painting," Melvin said. "As we were in our car heading back to Seminole, every one of us felt that we had just been in the presence of a great man."

Two of Melvin's historic meetings came about because of his friendship Judge Robert Henry.

In about 1992, when Senator Al Gore was running for president, Henry invited Melvin to his home to meet Senator Gore. When he arrived, it was not the presidential candidate he would meet, but his father.

Albert Gore was about 85 years old at the time. He had represented Tennessee in the United States Senate for many years and had been the Democratic leader in the Senate.

About 15 people were present, and they had an interesting visit with the guest of honor. The following story was related by Albert Gore:

The year was 1941 or 1942. President Roosevelt called into his office the leaders of Congress, including Gore, Speaker Barkley and others. The president told them he had a letter from Albert Einstein, notifying him that the Nazis were doing research on a terrible new weapon. Einstein told President Roosevelt that if the Nazis developed the weapon before the allies could develop a similar weapon, Einstein feared the Nazis would win the war.

"We must begin developing this weapon," Roosevelt told the senators and representatives. He asked them to find the money and to hide what they were doing by putting the appropriations on some obscure bill.

"No one on earth must know what we are doing," Roosevelt told Gore and the others.

Gore said the legislators did what the president asked and appropriated the money for the Manhattan Project.

"Now let's fast forward to 1945," Melvin said, retelling Gore's story.

*Senator Gore said he and two other senators were
making a trip into the Pacific to see first hand what was happening in the war. Senator Gore said they first went to Guam
and met with General Stillwell. There were troop ships and
soldiers everywhere, as far as the eye could see.*

*The senators were taken to the general's office, where the
walls were covered with maps. The general was preparing to
invade Japan, and he gave them the date, which was a
couple of weeks away. He pinpointed the places on the
maps where the invasion would actually take place.*

*"I asked General Stillwell what he thought the casualty
count would be," Gore said.*

*"I believe that we will have to kill a million Japanese,"
the general said. "And I fear that we will have 500,000
casualties."*

*The senators traveled on to the Philippines and met with
General Douglas MacArthur.*

*"By the time you get back to the mainland, the war will
be over," MacArthur told them.*

The senators could not believe what they were hearing,
Gore said, *"One day they were told the U.S. would have
500,000 casualties and a day later they were told the war
was about to end.*

*"A few days later we landed at the airport in San Fran-
cisco and the* San Francisco Chronicle *had published an
extra edition,"* Gore told the people at Judge Henry's that
day in 1992.

"The front page, in huge letters, had three words on it:

Atom Bomb Dropped."

Then Senator Gore said to Melvin and those other assembled at Robert Henry's house, "I was one of the persons responsible for the president getting the money to build the atomic bomb. But until that moment I had never heard of an atomic bomb. President Roosevelt did not tell us what the terrible weapon was that Einstein had written about.'"

A few days later when the senators arrived back in Washington, the headlines read "Japan Sues for Peace."

"I was so pleased that I had the opportunity to meet with Senator Gore and hear this story from his own lips," Melvin said.

Another "from the horse's mouth" story was when Henry invited Melvin to his house to meet Senator Tom Daschle, who was Senate Minority Leader; the year was about 1994.

"Senator Daschle told this story, which had taken place the week before he came to Oklahoma City," Melvin said.

In 1993, Czechoslovakia became the Czech Republic, but before that it was controlled by the Soviet Union. Vaclav Havel was a writer and was imprisoned for his political views. When he was sent to prison, he was not told how long he would be there – a month, a year or for life. He was imprisoned several times, the longest of which lasted four years.

When he was released, Havel was elected the last president of Czechoslovakia in 1989 and the first president of Czech Republic in 1993. Not long after the country became Czech Republic, United States President George Bush in-

vited Havel to Washington and gave a state dinner in his honor. Another person at the dinner was Senator Ted Kennedy.

Daschle told those gathered at Robert Henry's house that Havel went over to Senator Kennedy and said, "You are probably wondering why you were invited to this dinner." He said he'd asked that Kennedy be invited.

"When I was in prison, one of the books that was smuggled in to me was your brother's Profiles in Courage," Havel told the senator. "I was so inspired that I wanted to meet the President's brother."

Senator Kennedy asked President Havel if he'd ever been to Washington and the answer was no. Kennedy offered to give him a tour after dinner. He asked Havel where he'd like to go.

Havel wanted to visit the Capitol building, so they visited it; they went inside the Rotunda, where the only people left so late were security guards.

Then Havel asked to see the Jefferson Memorial and Kennedy took him there. The next place he wanted to see was the Lincoln Memorial.

"By this time it was 2:00 a.m.," Melvin was told. "President Havel went to the top of the steps of the Lincoln Memorial and recited from heart the Gettysburg Address. Senator Kennedy was amazed and President Havel said he had memorized this while in prison."

"Who would ever have imagined that the president of a former Iron Curtain country would be reciting the Gettysburg Address at the Lincoln Memorial at 2:00 a.m. to an audience of one?" Daschle concluded.

It was roughly this same time period when Melvin said he experienced one of the most memorable episodes of his life — speaking before 2,000 distinguished Americans in Washington, D.C. in honor of then-Senator David Boren when he was presented the Bryce Harlow Award for excellence in government relations.

"I received a letter from the Bryce Harlow banquet committee inviting me to be one of the speakers," Melvin said. "I accepted the invitation before they had time to change their minds."

The Bryce Harlow Award is presented annually in Washington, D.C. to a distinguished American. Harlow was an Oklahoman and a chief advisor to four American presidents. After his death, the Bryce Harlow Foundation was established.

"I was instructed to maintain secrecy because Senator Boren was not to know the identification of the speakers until the moment they stepped up to the podium," Melvin said.

Other banquet speakers included Senator Howard Baker of Tennessee, one of Melvin's heroes because of his part in the Watergate hearings; Senator Sam Nunn of Georgia, whose wisdom and bi-partisanship Melvin had long respected; Robert Henry, one of Boren and Melvin's close friends, who was, at the time, the dean of Oklahoma City University law school; and Denise Bode, then president of the Independent Petroleum Association of America and later Oklahoma Corporation Commissioner.

"The featured speaker was Senator Boren who, as usual, gave a brilliant speech," Melvin said.

The speakers were transported by limousine from their hotel to the banquet, being held at the famed Mayflower Hotel. "We were hidden in rooms until all the guests were seated, then quietly seated at tables in the rear of this huge banquet room," Melvin said.

At Melvin's table was Bode, who had been a longtime friend, and Bob Burke, who has written more about Oklahoma and Oklahomans than any other person in history.

Melvin and Jasmine and their daughter and son-in-law Marilyn and Bill Townsend with Senator David Boren in the Senate dining room in the early 1990s.

"When it was my turn to speak, I was introduced by Howard Baker and I was followed by Sam Nunn," Melvin said. "Wow! I don't recall if I was nervous or not. And I don't know how or why I was selected as one of the speakers. I suspect Molly Boren may have had something to do with that."

Melvin may be awed by the power and politics of Washington, but he is not one to be intimidated by important people. In 1999, Seminole County was redistricted into the same Congressional district as Oklahoma County. Ernest Istook represented the district.

"Congressman Istook was probably my least favorite among Oklahoma's congressional delegation," Melvin said. "There were two reasons — he was elected to that seat by defeating Mickey Edwards, a friend with whom I had traveled to Israel, and, second, because I disagreed with the majority of Congressman Istook's votes and I disagreed with almost 100 percent of his votes on social issues."

Because there were several plans on the table, Melvin had not worried much about his small town being thrown into the same congressional district as the big city. One day when he was in Oklahoma City for a meeting, Melvin was tapped on the shoulder and a deep voice asked, "Melvin, may I ask you a question?"

It was Congressman Istook, whom Melvin had not previously met.

"I have no idea how he knew who I was," Melvin said. "I immediately recognized him and responded, 'Certainly, Congressman.'"

Istook asked, "Melvin, would Seminole accept me as its congressman?"

"No, sir, we would not," Melvin said. "Seminole County is a rural county and we need to be in a congressional district with other rural counties. If we were in the district with Oklahoma City, Seminole would be like the tail on the Oklahoma City dog. I believe that we would have no representation at all. I believe that our economic development efforts would not receive the same assistance as economic development districts in Oklahoma City. Our hospital would not receive the same concern as would Oklahoma City hospitals. Our college would not receive the same attention as would Oklahoma City colleges. Seminole is an energy community," Melvin continued.

"Senator David Boren and then Congressman Wes Watkins were congressional leaders on energy issues. We need a congressman who understands energy issues and will help enact legislation helpful to the oil and gas industry. Congressman, those are major reasons why Seminole would not accept you as its congressman."

When Seminole and Pottawatomie counties were indeed redistricted into the Fifth Congressional District with Oklahoma City, Melvin became aware that, after the election, his town was going to be represented by the congressman whom he had "pretty much insulted."

Melvin invited Istook to be a speaker at the Seminole Chamber of Commerce's monthly Forum. Istook accepted.

Melvin meticulously planned the meeting. Speakers were given 20 to 25 minutes after a three-minute introduction.

Melvin asked the Chamber president to open the meeting 10 minutes early so he might give a 10-minute introduction of Istook.

The congressman sent a lengthy bio, which would have taken Melvin 10 minutes to read. Melvin picked out a few highlights and sped through those in about 60 seconds. He then related his previous conversation with the congressman, word for word.

In front of one of our largest Forum audiences ever, Melvin said, "Congressman, I challenge you to prove that I was wrong. Show us that Seminole's economic development efforts will receive the same attention as does Oklahoma City's. Show us that you will take care of our college in the same way that you take care of Oklahoma City's."

He told the congressman that the health of the oil and gas industry was vital to the Seminole community. He asked that Istook learn about the industry and become a leader and an advocate for energy.

"I think I probably blind-sided the Congressman more than he had ever been blind-sided before," Melvin said. "When I sat down, he got up and said the only thing he could think of to say — 'What would you like me to do on my second day in office?'"

Over the next several years, Melvin said, Istook did more for Seminole than any congressman within his memory.

"I am not belittling the work of the wonderful Wes Watkins," Melvin added. "And no one, to my mind, compares to David Boren. But he was a senator, not a congressman."

Istook was on the powerful appropriations committee and

headed several subcommittees.

"Wonderful things occurred in our community during the period we were represented by Congressman Istook," Melvin said. "Our education facilities, especially Seminole State College, received more help than ever before. Infrastructure was provided to our new industrial park. The city was helped in numerous ways. And indeed, he studied energy issues and became a leading advocate for this industry in Congress."

Istook often stopped by or called Melvin's office asking what he could do for Seminole. He opened a congressional office a half block from Melvin's office in Seminole. His staff person, Steve Jones, would come by and ask what the congressman could do for Seminole. Jones joined the Rotary Club and became a valuable part of the community.

"It was almost as though we had our own congressman with us full time," Melvin said. "With the exception of Senator Boren, this was, I believe, the first time there was ever a congressional office located within our city. More than one of the congressman's staff persons later told me that Congressman Istook was determined to meet the challenge I presented to him at that Forum in 1999."

To Melvin it seemed that Istook's votes on social issues were not as extreme as they had been previously.

"That was probably my imagination because I had come to know and like him," Melvin said. "He made me realize that there is more to a congressman than simply his voting record. How he looks after the community is of equal or possibly more importance. And we were taken care of in grand style. During this period, I was hoping that Oklahoma City residents were not becoming irritated with 'my' congressman because he spent so much time helping Seminole."

During Istook's last year in Congress, Melvin hosted a fundraiser for him in Seminole, encouraging his re-election.

"Prior to that time, if someone had suggested that I would be the sole host of a fundraiser for one of America's most conservative congressmen, I would have suggested that they must have been ingesting something that affected their capacity to be rational," Melvin joked.

But Istook's honeymoon with Seminole and Melvin ended a few months later when he called Melvin and asked what he thought about Istook running for governor.

"My response was, 'please don't!'" Melvin said. " 'I would hate to lose you as our congressman. And besides, you can't win.' I told him that I thought Brad Henry was a fine governor and that I would be strongly supporting his re-election. My friend, Ernest Istook, did run. And he was defeated by my friend, Brad Henry."

In relating his favorite memories, Melvin called the People to People tour of Russia one of his most memorable. The organization sends people to countries to help people in the same vocation or profession.

The two-week tour included 23 men, all involved in producing energy, and seven of them brought their spouses.

"The Iron Curtain had come down just a year or two before our trip," Melvin said. "Our job was to help bring the Russian energy industry into the 20th century."

After reading the agenda, which showed the visitors fly-ing from Moscow to Kazakhstan, then taking a helicopter to oilfields over the Caspian Sea, Melvin's first reaction was, "I'm not going."

"With acrophobia (an irrational fear of heights), there was no way I was going to take a helicopter for 200 miles," he said.

But Jasmine changed his mind.

"Mel, this is the opportunity for a trip of your lifetime," she said. "And don't worry; I will be holding your hand in the helicopter."

Melvin reluctantly agreed to go. They flew to New York City where they met the rest of the group.

"We were the only Oklahomans," Melvin said.

They were given orientation and instructions from the United States State Department.

"Some members of our group were hoping to make investments in Russian oil and gas," Melvin said. "The State Department representative told us that if we wanted to invest in Russian energy, we would first have to pay the bribe to Russian officials, but it would not be called a bribe. It would be called 'money to purchase a data package.' I asked how much the bribe would cost and the answer was, 'It usually averages about $1 million.'"

Melvin and Jasmine found the Russian people to be warm and wonderful, and very deprived. They traveled on a Finnish airline and landed in Moscow. There was not much motor traf-fic because there was very little gasoline available. Most service stations had none to sell. When one did, cars were lined up for a mile or more. The Morans visited various buildings in the Kremlin.

"This was an emotional experience for me," Melvin said. "My father was born in Latvia, which was controlled by Russia most of the time. And in Russia, a Russian is always a Russian. My father was afraid to visit his family in Latvia because he was afraid the Russians would not let him return to America. Yet here I was going through the buildings of the Kremlin."

They met with Russian officials, using an interpreter.

"We would speak in English and the interpreter would translate it into Russian," Melvin said. "And when the Russians spoke, the interpreter would translate their words into English."

Once in Moscow they had been meeting for about 30 minutes when one of the Russian officials looked at his watch and said in perfect English, "The time is getting late; let's speak English for the rest of the meeting."

"He spoke English as well as we did!" Melvin marveled.

Melvin and Jasmine found the food to be "generally awful." Fortunately they had taken a large jar of peanut butter with them, which went well with the "excellent" Russian bread.

They had heard that the Russian airline, Aeroflot, was one of the worst in the world. They found the reputation to be well-deserved on the day they were flying from Moscow to Tyumen in Siberia.

"It was suggested that we go to the airport early because one never knew when the plane would leave," Melvin said. "Sometimes it took off early. Usually they take off late. Often they don't take off at all because of lack of gasoline."

They found the airport's exterior to be in excellent condition; but inside, with rows and rows of neon lights on the ceiling, only two were working.

"It was so dark in the airport one could not even read," Melvin said. They found the restrooms to be "disgusting." They checked their luggage and were not given any receipts or tags. "We just hoped we'd see them again one day," Melvin said.

There were no assigned seats on the plane.

"Men trampled children and old ladies getting to the plane," he said. "After we got on, the seat backs would not come up. I put my arm on the armrest and it fell off."

The plane left about five hours late and the travelers landed in Tyumen at about 2:00 a.m. They were deplaned a half mile from the terminal, with almost no lights. Their bags were dumped onto the tarmac. In the dark, the group had to find their baggage and carry it the half mile to the terminal.

Because they were supposed to arrive in early evening, a welcome banquet had been planned. A large delegation had been waiting for them ever since.

"When we finally landed, we were told we must go to the banquet because these poor folks had been waiting for us for many hours," Melvin said. "We were completely exhausted, but we went to this banquet at about 3:00 a.m. They had entertainment — singers and dancers — and they were so wonderful and hospitable."

The people of Tyumen gave the travelers the grand tour the next day. They visited a factory that assembled pumping units for oil wells.

"We'd been told that 25 percent of all wells in Russia were shut in for lack of parts," Melvin said.

Russia had obtained its energy equipment from states that had been part of the Soviet Union, but they became independent and refused to sell parts to Russia without hard cash, which Russia did not have.

"I asked the manager of a plant that assembled pumping units how many shifts worked at that plant," Melvin said. "His response was 'one eight-hour shift.' And he said they put together eight pumping units each day.

"I asked, 'Why don't you work two or three shifts and put together more pumping units, since Russia needs them so badly?'"

The manager said there were not enough skilled workers.

"For example, we will be closed altogether tomorrow," the manager said. "The government has ordered us to shut down so all our workers can pick carrots."

The Americans were supposed to have stayed two days in Tyumen, but because their outgoing flight was being cancelled, they had to leave early. The group flew from Moscow to Kazakhstan where they were to take the helicopter to the new oilfield.

"As for Jasmine holding my hand, well that didn't happen," Melvin said. "While the men went to Kazakhstan, the women went to St. Petersburg to see beautiful artwork and jewelry."

The night before the trip, the group met with the helicopter owner, who asked the group leader how many were taking the helicopter trip. He was told 23 planned to go. The owner put that number in his calculator and multiplied it by the number of miles and said the cost would be $10,000.

The leader said, "But I already have an agreement with Mr. So-and-So and he said our cost would be $2,000." The owner put numbers in the calculator again and said, "The cost will be $8,000."

"Our leader said, 'For $8,000, we are not going anywhere,'" Melvin said.

"The owner again put numbers in his calculator and this time the answer was $2,000."

They boarded the old Army helicopter the next morning. There were no seats, only benches, and no seatbelts… "or anything like it," Melvin said. "I started psyching myself up. I said to myself, 'Helicopters don't go very high and they don't go very fast, so everything is going to be just fine.' I was feeling pretty good about everything. Just as we were lifting off the ground, one of the other energy executives started reciting the Lord's Prayer. I just about lost it."

Melvin's group traveled 200 miles over the Caspian Sea and the trip, thankfully, was uneventful.

In this oilfield there were 120 wells. With the oil, there was poison gas, which required a special refinery to refine the oil and take care of the poison gas. It took eight years to build the refinery and after it was built, it would only handle a quarter of the wells. So three-quarters of the field was shut down because of the lack of refining capacity.

Members of the tour group were given gas masks because

of the poison gas, with instructions on use in Russian.

"Fortunately there were no fatalities," Melvin said.

At the time there were 30 new wells being drilled in the field, but only one drilling rig was operating because the workers for the other 29 rigs were on strike. They had not been paid in months. The Americans found that the oilfield equipment, including the drilling rigs, were technically about 75 years behind the United States.

"The trip was quite an experience," Melvin said. "And it made us realize more than ever how fortunate we are to live in the United States."

The Seminole delegation to the 2007 dedication of the USS Oklahoma *memorial dedication in Honolulu, Hawaii, included, from right, Melvin and Jasmine Moran, Dale and Marci Donaho, and State Representative Ryan Kiesel and his wife, Allison.*

Another historic trip in the lives of Melvin and Jasmine was the 2007 dedication of a memorial for the 429 sailors who lost their lives at Pearl Harbor on the U.S.S *Oklahoma*.

The 12 speakers at the dedication included the governors of Oklahoma and Hawaii, members of Congress from Oklahoma and Hawaii, several admirals, several survivors of the U.S.S *Oklahoma*, children of sailors who were killed during the bombing, and the architect who designed the memorial.

"All the speakers were very eloquent," Melvin said. "The elected officials spoke of the need for the memorial. The survivors and children of those who died spoke of the closure that the memorial provided and the architect told us about the design for the memorial."

Architect Don Beck from Oklahoma went to Pearl Harbor for inspiration before beginning the memorial. He stood in the very spot where the memorial was to be placed. A battleship floated by. The sailors on board were "railing" – all standing in formation next to the rails wearing their dress whites.

Beck took his inspiration from the white-clad sailors and erected round white marble pillars, 10 feet tall by four inches in diameter, to symbolize the 429 who died in the bombing. The pillars top large horizontal slabs of black granite, similar to the Vietnam Memorial in Washington, D.C.

Also attending from Seminole were Marci and Dale Donaho, Sheila Weems, and State Representative Ryan Kiesel and his wife Allison.

"Approximately 600 sailors survived the sinking of the ship," Melvin said. "Of that number, approximately 80 were still alive on December 7, 2007. And 16 of those were present for the dedication."

The Morans had the opportunity to visit with several of the survivors, including George Smith who was one of the ship's cooks. He was the youngest sailor on the ship, just 17 years old.

At the time of the attack, Smith had just finished his shift and was down below changing clothes. As the Pearl Harbor attack was taking place, Smith looked out of a porthole and saw a Japanese plane heading toward the ship. The plane was flying very low and dropped a torpedo. While the torpedo was on its way, the Japanese pilot lifted his cockpit hatch, saw Smith, and then waved as the plane flew over the ship. The torpedo struck the ship.

CHAPTER TWENTY-ONE

The Highest Honor

"This is the kind of man spoken of in the book of
Ruth in whom the sovereign 'delighteth to honor.'"
— Robert Henry

For a man so well known and respected, it was
only a matter of time — Melvin Moran was named
to the Oklahoma Hall of Fame in 1997.

"I believe the Hall of Fame is the highest honor
an Oklahoman can receive," Melvin said. "The first
congratulatory call I received was from Gene Rainbolt.
I thanked him and told him I was both humbled and
proud. And I told him that, at the same time, I was
sad and felt guilty because he was much more deserving of the honor than I." Rainbolt was inducted
into the Oklahoma Hall of Fame two years later.

Robert Henry wrote,

"A successful businessman, Melvin has re
turned his success generously to his community
– his state, nation and world. An expert on oil
and gas issues, [Melvin] has consistently donated
that experience to public policy makers who
must base that policy, as well as they can, on the
eccentricities of those issues. A devout member
of his own religious faith, he has worked tire-
lessly to allow others to be devoted to their
faiths. A serious leader, he knows the importance

Melvin Moran was inducted into the Oklahoma Hall of Fame in 1997; his wife Jasmine was at his side.

BELOW: Left to right, Robert Henry, Jan Ralls, Jasmine Moran, and Melvin Moran. Introducing Melvin at his Hall of Fame induction was Robert Henry, then OCU Law School Dean. In 2008, Henry was also named to the Hall of Fame.

of the laughter of children and the importance of their usually kind, inquisitive natures. This is the kind of man spoken of in the book of Ruth in whom the sovereign 'delighteth to honor.'"

"The six months between being selected for the Hall of Fame and my induction were the most memorable months of my life," Melvin said.

As honorees do, Melvin invited friends and family from all over the world. Virtually everyone came: college friends, officers with whom he had served in the Air Force in England, and his relatives, including three families from England.

"Since folks came from around the country and beyond, most of them spent a full week in Oklahoma," Melvin said. "So we had parties with all these wonderful friends and families for a week. What a glorious time it was!"

The inductees were to wear tails. Melvin's tux had no tails so he had to rent one. A week prior to the event he went to Oklahoma City and a tailor measured him for the tux. He picked it up about two hours before the ceremony.

Jasmine accompanied him and insisted that Melvin try the tux on.

"I told her that a professional tailor had measured me and that there was no need, but she insisted," Melvin said.

He tried it on and came out of the dressing room to show her.

Military buddy Bob Scholtens and his wife Joan visit the Morans in Seminole for Melvin's 1997 Hall of Fame induction.

Daughter Elisa was among the family members attending Melvin's Hall of Fame induction.

Congratulating Melvin on his induction into the Hall of Fame is his longtime good friend, Cecil Sullivan.

"I told her it fit just fine and she told me to turn around," Melvin said. "I told her there was no need, it fit just fine."

But when he did turn around, there was a hole in the seat of the pants as big as a basketball.

"I hadn't noticed it when I put on the pants," he said. "I shudder to think what could have happened if I hadn't tried it on."

The tux rental clerks were embarrassed when Melvin showed them the hole, and were able to find him another pair of pants.

"I don't know if my speech was memorable or not, but if I had come out wearing that first pair of pants, my induction into the Oklahoma Hall of Fame would indeed have been remembered," Melvin said, laughing.

As humble as always, Melvin said his achievements were small compared to the other inductees. In addition to Melvin, the 1997 class was comprised of W.W. Allen, CEO of Phillips Petroleum; Ann Alspaugh, Oklahoma City arts philanthropist; Vince Gill, renowned country music performer; Tony Hillerman, best-selling and nationally-recognized author; and General Dennis Reimer, chief of staff of the United States Army.

Mistress of Ceremonies for the induction was former Miss America Shawntel Smith, who Melvin visited with that night and later nominated to fill a vacancy on the museum's board of directors. After serving for several years and becoming friends, the Morans attended her wedding in Sallisaw.

"Of all the six Hall of Fame inductees that year, I believe that I had the least credentials of any of them," Melvin said. "But my presenter, Robert Henry, was so eloquent, and he made me appear worthy of induction."

"If a person selects you to introduce them at the Hall of Fame induction, it's a mixed blessing," said Henry. "It's a great honor, but trying to encapsulate Melvin Moran in three to five minutes is difficult. I did what they told me to and it irritated me because others didn't. I got mine down to the limit and others didn't. It miffed me because I thought Melvin was a bigger deal than some of the others."

Presentation of Melvin Moran for Induction into the Oklahoma Hall of Fame

By Robert Henry

In a portion of the Talmud called 'Sayings of the Fathers,' the rabbis teach: who is wise? He who learns from every person. Who is honored? He who honors his fellow man.

Melvin Moran has learned and now teaches this lesson, especially with respect to children. But his founding – with his wife Jasmine – of perhaps the world's finest children's museum is just the culmination of a philanthropy that has also included ministering to the elderly and lonely by establishing an annual Christmas dinner which serves hundreds; providing time and funds to Seminole State College and Ben-Gurion University; advising and financially assisting the once national champion and still powerful Seminole High School debate team; funding scholarships for the Oklahoma Arts Institute; and donating expertise and money to virtually every good cause brought to his attention.

No wonder the Oklahoma Chapter of the National Society of Fundraising Executives named him 'Philanthropist of the Year' or that his wife Jasmine simply says he's 'generous to a fault.'

Melvin's business acumen has led him to be the managing partner of Moran Oil Enterprises and Moran-K Oil, companies that engage in production and exploration of oil and gas.

His knowledge on these matters caused him to be selected president of the Oklahoma Independent Petroleum Association and named a board member of both the Independent Petroleum Association of America and the Mid-Continent Oil and Gas Association.

Indeed his expertise in oil and gas has led to his consultation by the Governor's Advisory Council on Energy, the State Board of Equalization, the Secretary of Energy and President Clinton.

His petroleum prognostications have been printed in numerous magazines and journals including *Fortune*, *Time*, *Business Week*, *The New York Times*, *The Chicago Tribune* and *The London Financial Times*.

And Melvin is an admirer of politicians, perhaps because he has labored himself in that vineyard. A seven-term city councilman, he was also vice mayor and finally mayor of his hometown of Seminole; he has also been appointed to numerous state boards by four governors, and has served as county or state chairman for candidates for senator, governor, lieutenant governor, attorney general and Congress.

He has also been an unofficial emissary of the Republic of Israel, hosting and visiting major political, intellectual and military figures from that country.

But it is the Jasmine Moran Children's Museum that is his first love. He is hands-on; he can be found there almost every day, welcoming the more than 75,000 visitors, mostly children, who come each year. More than just a focus for learning science and tradition, the museum is a center of children's creativity, understanding, in the words of Albert Einstein, that 'Imagination is more important than knowledge.' Perhaps Melvin understands the imaginative needs of children because he himself has a childlike faith, a childly tolerance and a childish curiosity.

This evening I am honored to present this producer of oil and adviser to presidents and prime ministers, this donor to all good charities and kingmaker of politicians; this financier of a brighter future for Oklahoma; and this curator of children's smiles... Melvin Moran.

When Henry placed the earthen red ribbon holding the Hall of Fame medallion around Melvin's neck, Melvin thanked the museum's staff, board, volunteers, and donors, and introduced his family. He talked about his beloved Seminole. "In our city, community service is infectious. Almost everyone has caught it. I hope they never find a cure." And he encapsulated his own self-effacing personality in his words, "I don't know if I'm deserving, but I'm very appreciative."

In all things, Melvin is humble. He may be lauded by the likes of a chief judge of the 10th Circuit Court of Appeals, a United States senator, and the governor of the state of Oklahoma, but he always somehow finds ways to turn the praise to others.

When faced with recognition, Melvin named three men as the mentors of his adult life.

"David Boren is the most inspiring person I have ever known in the political and public service areas," Melvin said. "I am proud to have supported him in his various elections. At the same time, in addition to inspiring me, he opened up so many doors for me. His influence and his friendship have led me to become friends with so many governors, congresspersons, and numerous elected and appointed officials in Oklahoma, to so many senators and other governmental officials."

Gene Rainbolt is another who has inspired Melvin because of his dedication to Oklahoma.

"Gene has also opened up many doors and caused me to meet so many persons involved in Oklahoma's civic activities," Melvin said. When Gene was state Chamber president, he appointed Melvin to the Chamber board. When Gene was active in the Oklahoma Academy, he caused Melvin to become a member of the board of directors. When Gene founded BancFirst, he invited Melvin to become one of the founding directors.

"Gene is a mentor and a teacher," Melvin said. "I learned from Gene about banking and became involved in numerous state activities because of his influence."

Milt Phillips inspired Melvin to become civically active in his community.

"I was constantly amazed by his insight and his intelligence," Melvin said. "During my lifetime in Seminole, Milt was Seminole's number one civic leader, in my opinion. He deserves much of the credit for the great strides that have been made in our community."

The Golden Years

"It was a wonderful evening, one that I will never forget for the rest of my life."

— Melvin Moran

In the year 2000, Melvin celebrated his 70th birthday. Jasmine conspired with their children, Melvin's office personnel, and museum director Marci Donaho on a guest list which included family, friends, and those who have served with Melvin on a variety of boards.

"Over several months there were a number of times when I would walk into the house and find Jasmine on the phone and she would immediately hang up," Melvin said. "But I never noticed. Though I am naïve, there were some comments made by some of the invitees which did make me a little suspicious."

But the day of his birthday came and went with only a small office party, the kind they have for everyone's birthday. On his birthday, Bob and Barbara Jones and Dale and Marci Donaho took the Morans out to dinner.

"So my suspicions were unfounded, I thought," Melvin said.

Two weeks after his birthday, his cousin Norman Landa from Dallas called and said he had an extra ticket for the University of Oklahoma football game.

CHAPTER TWENTY-TWO

"Without hesitation, my response was 'yes, thank you!'" Melvin said. "My suspicions of a surprise party immediately returned. I thought Norman would invite me to meet him at some address in Norman and that would be the site of my birthday party. Instead, Norman said he would FedEx my ticket and meet me at the stadium. So much for my suspicions."

In Norman, Melvin parked a mile northwest of the stadium. Landa said he had parked a mile southeast of the stadium. But when the game was over he said he would walk Melvin back to his car.

"I wondered why he would do that," Melvin said. "This would be literally miles out of his way. I thought, 'Aha! When I get to my car, a bunch of people will have been hiding in the back of my car and they will all stand up and yell Happy Birthday!'"

Melvin's 70th birthday in 2000 was held at the Jasmine Moran Children's Museum. Daughter Elisa prepared a display commemorating Melvin's love of golf.

THIS BALL IS GENUINE SCOT
IT'S TRAVELED FAR AND WIDE
INTO A ST. ANDREWS' SAND TRAP
WHERE IT WOUNDED MELVIN'S PRIDE!

THIS ONE TOWERED A
JUST AS PRETTY AS
WHEN MELVIN LET IT FLY
AND IT LANDED IN A

NEITHER SNOW NOR RAIN
NOR SLEET NOR HAIL
KEEPS MELVIN FROM GOLF
AND HIS LEGENDARY TA

SO MANY GOLF BAL
SO LITTLE SATISFA
MOST OF THEM ARE
STILL "MISSING IN

But Landa walked Melvin to his car, said goodbye, and walked away.

"I arrived back in Seminole shortly after 4:00 p.m.," Melvin said. "When I return from out of town, I frequently stop at the museum and I walk around and watch the kids. As I drove up to the museum, I noticed that there was a closed sign on the door. I wondered why, because the museum doesn't close until 5:00 p.m. At the same time, there were lots of cars. That didn't add up — closed, but lots of cars in the parking lot?"

Melvin used his key to open the front door.

"As I did, I saw lots of people scattering as fast as they could," Melvin said. "At that point, the light dawned and I said to myself, 'I should not have stopped here today.'"

In the museum at that time were dozens of family members finishing decorations. So Melvin's surprise birthday party took place in the museum a couple of hours later. Hundreds of friends and family members from all over the country were there.

"It was a wonderful evening, one that I will never forget for the rest of my life," Melvin said. "I particularly remember one couple at the party. They seemed to be having the very best time. However, I have no idea who they were. Neither did Jasmine. But I am glad they enjoyed themselves."

In 2005, after 31 years at 2300 Morningside, the Morans contracted with local builder Keith Shaw for a new home at 1023 Sterling Drive.

"We wanted to downsize, and the house on Morningside was a two-story which was hard for Jasmine," Melvin said.

Melvin visited with a host of family and friends at his 70th birthday party.

At Melvin's 70th birthday, son David read a proclamation from the governor.

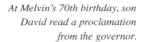

To make maneuvering around the house easier for Jasmine, the Morans began looking at house plans.

"Jasmine had listed her priorities and she indicated that she wanted a bathroom near the kitchen," Melvin said.

On a Sunday morning Shaw called and told them their plans were completed and he wanted their final okay before proceeding. He dropped off the plans that afternoon, immediately after dropping off house plans for Dan and Deanna Hamilton's new home.

The Morans looked over the blueprints and Jasmine asked, "Where is my bathroom near the kitchen?"

"I can't find it, but I know it's there," said Melvin.

"Well, I am not signing anything until I see my bathroom," she said.

That evening Melvin called Shaw and asked about the bathroom.

"I remember Jasmine being emphatic about it and I'm sure it's there," Shaw said.

He asked Melvin to bring in the blueprints in the morning and he would point out the bathroom.

"I took in the blueprints and told Keith everything looked great except I wanted him to assure me that the bathroom was there," Melvin said.

Shaw took at look at the blueprints and said, "Melvin this isn't your home. I accidentally left you the blueprints for Dan Hamilton's house."

"I saw Dan the following week and told him that Jasmine and I very much liked his new home except for the fact that he doesn't have a bathroom by the kitchen," Melvin said.

CHAPTER TWENTY-THREE

A Self Description

"I believe in taking care of people not as well off as we are, Social Security, welfare."

— Melvin Moran

So who is this man named Melvin Moran? He's a small five-foot-seven-inch man with gray hair and glasses. He wears mostly polo shirts and knit slacks, clothes that his wife has chosen for him. Sometimes he wears jeans and tennis shoes, but mainly preferring to wear shoes he does not have to tie.

"I hate shopping," he said. "When I shop, I have tunnel vision. I go in, pick up what I need and get out. I almost run."

He is a devout Jew, a devoted husband, and a proud father and grandfather. He is a registered Democrat, though he frequently votes Republican.

"From the time I first registered to vote, I have always been a registered Democrat," Melvin said. "Most likely I registered as a Democrat because that was the party of my parents. I have remained a Democrat because the platforms of the Democratic party more nearly match my beliefs. I believe in taking care of people not as well off as we are, Social Security, welfare. However, I strongly believe that the person matters much more than the party and I have voted for and supported many Republican candidates and office holders."

Melvin describes himself as "socially moderate and fiscally conservative. We need to create jobs and business to help people that way. I vote both parties, but most often for Democrats."

He loves golf and tries to play nine holes a week, but it is "usually about 18 holes a month," he said. He is an avid reader, mostly newspapers and magazines, reading four newspapers a day. "I also read *TIME* Magazine, *NewsWeek*, *Readers Digest*, and oil and gas magazines," Melvin said. "I'm a fast reader, but I have little time for books." He likes music from the 1940s and 1950s: the Dorseys and Henry James. "I don't like loud music or music that I can't understand the words," he said.

He likes bland food. "I'm a meat-and-potatoes man," he said. "Jasmine introduced me to fruits and vegetables and I eat them to look after my health. For religious reasons I don't eat pork or shellfish. My favorite food is salmon croquettes. My mother made them and so does Jasmine." He does not drink much, usually just a glass of wine on religious occasions, saying alcohol does not taste good. "I sipped beer in college, but I didn't like it," he said. "There is no possibility of my getting drunk. I'm fine after one drink and I go to sleep after the second."

He is almost obsessive about time management. "Every day there is more on my schedule than I can do," he said. "I work fast to get it all done. It gives me great pleasure to mark things off the list. And I'm a good delegater."

Melvin's worst setbacks were the death of his parents and his worst fear is about being physically incapacitated. "I worry about physical ailments and being incapacitated," he said. "I've been blessed with good health and a good memory. I can introduce 70 or 100 people at our board meetings and recite where they all work and live."

And he plans never to retire. "I love to go to work," he said. "I like spending part of each day at the museum and in civic activities. I have to have something to look forward to in the morning."

"Melvin couldn't retire," Jasmine said. "I told him that if he did, one of us would die and it wouldn't be me. I'd probably kill him. He'd be sitting around agitated all the time because he loves to work."

If this is how Melvin describes himself, then how does the rest of the world see him? "Melvin Moran has universal appeal to do-gooders, that's for sure," said his longtime friend Robert Henry. "Part-time do-gooders like me are captivated by full-time do-gooders like him. He is a do-gooder on stilts. I am not objective about Melvin Moran. He's made a great impact on my life. He has directed my path."

His state representative, Ryan Kiesel, said he gets short, hand-written notes and e-mail from Melvin all the time, usually commending him on something he has done or alerting him to issues of animal cruelty or abuse.

"In the legislature, you have to make tough votes," Kiesel said. "And there will always be someone walking around the floor, whispering in your ear, 'This will make you big,' or 'You could lose an election over this.' You wouldn't believe the hateful e-mails I get and usually not from my constituents."

With all that going on, Kiesel will hear a "ding" and find

an e-mail from Melvin: "You're doing a good job." "Thank you so much for your vote on this, or your opposition to that." "Jasmine and I are proud of you."

"To get notes like that from someone like him – it keeps you going up there," Kiesel said. "I've saved all his e-mails. I wrote him back once and told him that he couldn't realize how much his words and confidence meant to me."

In January, 2007, Kiesel had an extra ticket for the governor's inauguration and invited Melvin to join him. They met first on the House floor.

"There was a line that formed to speak to him, like he was a celebrity," Kiesel said. "Even people who didn't know him personally wanted to meet him. And not to get contributions either. Every person had such nice things to say about him.

"You think everyone in Seminole knows him, but you should see him in Tulsa. All the leaders in the state, in the community, in business, they all know him. And nobody calls him Mr. Moran. If anybody calls him Mr. Moran, they haven't met him yet."

Kiesel talked about the wonderful experiences he has had serving in the state legislature and said one of the greatest benefits was getting to know Melvin.

"He's the consummate Oklahoman," he said. "There is a gap in modern Oklahoma history between Will Rogers and Wiley Post and the present. If you ask people who best represents Oklahoma's spirit, they say Shannon Miller or Toby Keith. You have to either do somersaults or sing country music.

"As far as politicians, society is usually looking to tear

them down. You can look all over and you'd be hard pressed to find anyone who would want to denigrate or bring Melvin Moran down.

"He's a Renaissance Man of Oklahoma history."

State Senator Harry Coates, one of the Republicans that Melvin has backed, says Melvin is the kindest person he knows.

"My dad was always so complimentary of Melvin and how he led his life," Coates said. "For years I taught a Sunday School class of junior and senior high boys. Many times we would talk about current events and how they related to Biblical teachings. It always worked better if they could relate what we were talking about to someone in our community. Many times I used Melvin, a Jew, as an example of how we as Christians should live our lives."

Coates said he is another who has never heard Melvin speak unkindly, even though he has been tested. He referred to a time when a vocal advocate of cockfighting attempted to bring a vote to the floor of the Senate a bill that would legalize cockfighting.

"I got an e-mail from Melvin saying that legislator was a BAD man," Coates said. "Anyone else would have said 'that @#&*@##$ [person] is a crazy man!'"

From a business standpoint, Coates said Melvin would not do business with anyone he feels is of poor character or with whom he has to have an agreement beyond that of a handshake.

"How remarkable is it that a man of means and position puts honesty and integrity above all the contracts that may be generated by our great legal minds?" he said.

Coates said he is so grateful to be involved in the Children's Museum. He feels that the character and quality of the individuals Melvin drew together to make the museum one of Oklahoma's major tourist attractions is simply amazing.

"Many of those individuals are very powerful leaders, who I have an opportunity to be around on a regular basis now, but were it not for Melvin, I would not have ever been able to be in the Senate," Coates said. He believes the turning point in his career was when Melvin made it public that he would support Coates, a Republican.

"I owe a lot to Melvin Moran and am always so proud to tell others that he and I have a personal friendship," Coates said. "Other than my family, Melvin is the one person in the world I would least want to disappoint. I respect this man more than I can say."

The legislators' views of Melvin Moran are mirrored by his opinion of them.

"I believe that Seminole is the home of two of the very best legislators in the entire legislature," Melvin said recently.

He thinks that if he were a legislator, his votes would coincide with Kiesel's more than with any other legislator. But if he were a legislator, Melvin said he would want to be a Harry Coates.

"I would hope that I would vote my convictions and for what I believe was right regardless of the position of my party," Melvin said. "Harry does that every time."

Melvin's involvement in politics could impact Oklahoma

in the long run, believes First Lady Kim Henry.

"Melvin is one of those individuals who really looks at the person running," she said. "That's what he is interested in: getting good people elected to office. He is one of the few who are very active in politics with no pre-set agenda. He wants to be involved in electing an honest person, one of quality."

David Boren, who has known Melvin since Boren was a teen and was helped by Melvin in campaigns from state representative to U.S. senator, believes that no one in the history of Seminole has been more dedicated to his community.

"Melvin is the kind of person who could live anywhere and handle his investments wherever he wanted to be, but he chose Seminole," Boren said. It is something the Seminole native understands well.

"I'm from Seminole no matter where I happen to be living temporarily," Boren said. "I'm stationed in different places, but I feel that identity with the community just like Melvin does. He understands my love for it."

For a community to be strong, Boren said there must be someone to take responsibility when people say, "Someone ought to do this or that."

"Melvin has done that," Boren said. "He assumes responsibility for other people and their well-being and has literally dedicated his life to Seminole. The town wouldn't be anything like it is today without his involvement."

He talked about Melvin's contributions to school, to economic development, the college, the hospital, and, of course, the museum. He pointed out that Melvin was always the peacemaker, bringing people together, working together for the good of the community.

"He helped create a community spirit of tolerance in Seminole," Boren said. "He represents tolerance and kindness towards others, whether they are the same political persuasion or religion, and he demonstrates respect to everyone. He is a role model of generosity, respect, and tolerance.

"Seminole has a very special spirit that doesn't exist in many other cities and towns," Boren said. "I think you can trace much of that back to Melvin."

Boren, through his years in politics and now as president of the University of Oklahoma, said he feels fortunate to have shared a friendship with Melvin.

"He is a wonderful person to go to for advice," Boren said. "Very often when I was in the governor's office and in Washington, I went to him. He is a great listener and observer and I knew he'd tell me what people were really thinking and saying, the unvarnished truth. He was not afraid to tell me when he thought I was wrong and that's an important quality in a friend and advisor. He'd put it in the most kind way, usually like a question: have you thought about this or that? He didn't just say I was wrong. It was always a series of questions."

Boren worries about what will happen to Seminole after Melvin is gone, and believes that Melvin might prove irreplaceable to the community.

"There's just never going to be another Melvin Moran," he said. "I think it will take several people to take his place when we no longer have him around. Molly and I have talked about that – what will happen to Seminole when Melvin and Jasmine aren't there.

"Melvin would be confident, saying there are lots of good people who will become leaders, but my guess is that it would take a good half dozen leaders, probably people who have been inspired by his example, dedication, and energy."

Melvin's old high school friend says Melvin's whole life has been a "contradiction."

"In high school, he didn't play football or softball," said Maynard Ungerman of Tulsa. "We never thought he cared much about it. But then, low and behold, the next thing he's doing is traveling Europe and playing table tennis on a championship military team.

"In high school, if we met girls, he was the last one to go after them," Ungerman continued. "He wasn't the best looking, he wasn't a great dancer or a good driver or even a good talker. He certainly wasn't the best athlete. We were always making sure he had dates, while all of us thought we were the nearest thing to Errol Flynn.

"Then when we grew up, we all married and Mel gets this gorgeous British actress with loads of personality to boot.

"He's always so happy about what he's doing that he falls into good things. He's still a kid at heart."

Another high school friend, Mervin Aptak, regrets that there is so little time for the two of them to get together.

"Melvin was always a bright, wonderful guy," Aptak said. "We went into different businesses and both worked lots of hours. I don't see him or talk to him as often as I'd like, but my feelings for him now are as strong as they were back then."

The man who some say is Melvin's best friend is Cecil Sullivan. The two meet at 10:30 a.m. every day for tea at a local restaurant, Lunch 'n' Such, and talk over matters of the world.

"Melvin and I are pretty different," Sullivan said. "He's Rotary and I'm Lions Club. He's Jewish and I'm Church of Christ, which is pretty much as polarized as possible. He's Democrat and I'm a rebel. He's always optimistic and I'm pessimistic.

"We've been best friends for years."

He admits that they sometimes disagree.

"We talk about everything," Sullivan said. "Political, civic. We get extremely personal. We don't hold back. Even our wives don't know some of the things we talk about. I know a lot of his secrets… but I'm not telling. We disagree a lot but neither of us holds grudge.

"Melvin," Sullivan said, "is extremely busy.

"I have to fit my schedule to his," he said. "He'll say, 'I will meet you at the golf course at 12:46. We've been playing golf together forever, but he's never going to be much of a golfer."

Sullivan said the worst thing he can say about Melvin is that sometimes he will not make a decision.

"I tell him to get off the fence, but he still won't make a decision because he's afraid it might hurt someone," Sullivan said.

A person would never know how well off Melvin is, Sullivan said, because, although he lives well, he lives simply. He will not buy a Cadillac because it is a status symbol. And he will not buy a foreign car. His last car had more than 100,000 miles on it and the tires were beginning to blow out before Sullivan convinced him it was time to get another car.

"He didn't want to, but I told him that Jasmine worries about him when he's on the road in that old car," Sullivan said. "So he went down and told them what he wanted. He has to have all the gadgets. He told them 'Cecil will be down to make the deal for me.' I do his bartering for him. I asked to see what they were doing for him and they had actually given him a heck of a deal, so I okayed it."

Melvin's friend Marci Donaho said Melvin read the entire 493 pages of the new car's manual.

"Nobody does that," she said.

Several mentioned Melvin's driving; apparently he drives fast and is easily distracted while on the road.

"I know he has a guardian angel with him in the car," Donaho said. "He could be a Nascar driver; the other drivers would be fearful and let him pass."

Robert Henry's one great worry about Melvin is that he needs to get somebody to drive him. "You can't keep working that hard and going to all these meetings," Henry said. "I mean, he's a young 78, but that doesn't matter."

After a recent museum meeting at the new Skirvin Hotel, Melvin planned to drive back to Seminole. The hotel is where he and Jasmine spent their wedding night and Henry encouraged Melvin to stay over.

"He's so frugal in his personal life," Henry said. "When he agreed, I took it as a personal triumph. I sent him a bottle of champagne."

Sullivan said Melvin told him once that he wants to live well and the rest of his money he would gladly just give away.

"And he does give a lot away," Sullivan said. "He can be such a patsy. Every sob story that comes to his office gets something. I've seen him give away $20 or $25 from his pocket and never even make a note of it."

"Melvin is very generous and dynamic," said his brother, Sid, "giving away much of his money.

"I say he needs to be careful, no matter what his net worth is," Sid said. "But I always followed his footsteps and admired him, and not only his accomplishments, but his ethical standards.

"He is the leader of the whole family. He helps all the cousins. He brings people from all over the world so they can be at the family reunions. He is very generous."

His sister Jeannie Tiras said there is nothing in the world she would not do for her brother.

"I don't know where he gets this incredible energy," she said. "Neither of our parents had it. Sid and I are jealous of it."

Melvin's office staff knows Melvin in a different way – but they seem to adore him.

Sherry Cowan has worked as a secretary in his office for 18 years and in the Morans' home before that.

"Melvin is one of a kind," she said. "I love him dearly and am blessed to have worked with him all these years. I can't say enough good about either him or Jasmine. If everybody were the kind of people that Melvin and Jasmine are, the world would not be in the shape it is today."

Her favorite stories about Melvin include the time his

office flooded and everything had to be moved into another room. He had to work from the new office for several weeks while his was being gutted, cleaned, and re-roofed.

"He was just lost," she said. "He didn't even have a desk, just a table by the window. And everything was covered in water.

"I remember him coming to my office with this pathetic little look on his face, his shoulders all rounded over, looking so sad," Cowan said. "He asked, 'do you know where my little wet calculator is?' and I'll never forget that little puppy dog look as he followed me through the office to find it. I just felt so sorry for him."

Melvin's fear of heights is something that is not well known, but Cowan has seen it in action.

She was working at the Moran house on Morningside Drive, and an upstairs bathroom window screen was flapping in the wind.

"I tried to fix it from the inside, but I couldn't," she said. "I told Melvin and he said he'd get a ladder. When he put it up, he said, 'I'll hold it while you climb up there.'"

They wrangled about who had to go up the ladder until Melvin said, "I can't go up there."

"I'm afraid of heights," Cowan said. "I have a horrible inner-ear equilibrium problem and I can be standing on solid ground and just fall down when it hits.

"But I guess I'm not as afraid of heights as Melvin. He and Jasmine each held a side of the ladder for me while I climbed up. As I got higher and higher, I kept having to stop and rest more often. But I did it."

Melvin has talked about how unobservant he can be and Cowan said she had seen that a couple of times. Once after a fundraiser for Robert Henry, Melvin started moving the chairs back to their regular places. While Cowan was cleaning up, Melvin stopped her and asked about one of the chairs.

"I told him it came from his bedroom, on Jasmine's side of the bed," she said. "It matched the drapes. He asked me not to tell her and I never did."

Not all that long ago, the office staff decided to give the office a little makeover and Cowan went out to buy some wooden bookshelves to replace the old metal ones that had been in the office since it was opened in the 1950s.

"After a week or 10 days, Melvin came in and asked, 'How long have I had those?'" Cowan said, laughing. "He said, 'Please don't tell me they've been there for a long time.'"

Office manager Barbara Jones has been friends with Melvin and Jasmine for more than 37 years, employed by Melvin for over 16 years.

"To really know Melvin, you need to work with him on a daily basis," she said. "I have never been associated with anyone more organized and in control of his life. And his sense of humor is revealed in his outstanding ability to tell funny stories about himself."

Once, she remembered, Melvin decided to film some of the funny stories for a family reunion and asked for her help. But first she started laughing, then he started laughing and neither one could finish the filming because they were laughing so hysterically.

"We both decided it would be better to tell the stories in a live setting," she said.

Her husband, Bob Jones, believes he owes his life to Melvin.

"Everyone who knows Melvin knows how persistent he can be to get you to do something," Jones said. In 2006, Lifeline Screening sent an application to Melvin to have an ultrasound to determine blockage in arteries or if an aneurysm was present.

"He gave the application to Barbara and insisted that we have this screening," Jones said. "Reluctantly, I went. What they found that day was an abdominal aortic aneurysm. That afternoon I was in the Oklahoma Heart Hospital making arrangements for more tests and surgery. If not for Melvin's insistence and concern, I might not be here today."

Jones first knew Melvin in 1969 when Jones was hired as Chamber of Commerce manager.

"Being a 30-year-old Chamber manager with no experience in community development, the Seminole business community took a chance that I could do the job," Jones said. "The burden was placed on Melvin and other community leaders to provide the leadership I needed."

Jones was a constant visitor to Melvin's office. When he needed help, Melvin was always there to provide solutions or ideas on startup of new programs.

He remembered the 1973 Gridiron Show, a major fundraising event written and directed by Melvin and Jasmine for 60 cast members. It was so successful that Melvin produced another show in 1975.

"These two events did wonders in bringing the community

together," Jones said. "It gave the cast an opportunity to make friends and the motivation for working together to solve many community problems."

Jones also was involved when Melvin and Jasmine returned from Michigan with the idea for a children's museum.

"The Jasmine Moran Children's Museum is a tribute to Melvin's determination to complete any task he sets his heart on," Jones said.

"There are not enough words to explain what Melvin means to this community and the state of Oklahoma. Everyone knows that Melvin is the person to contact on any subject, big or small. No one is more respected than Melvin Moran."

Jones' funny story about Melvin is a night when they went out to dinner, then returned to the Jones' home for cake and coffee. Melvin excused himself to visit the restroom. As they visited, they noticed that Melvin had been gone for a very long time. Thirty minutes later, Melvin returned, but no one dared to ask him what took so long.

"After awhile, Melvin couldn't stand it any longer," Jones said. "He said, 'Don't you want to know what happened to me?'

"We all said yes and he said, 'The bathroom door jammed and I couldn't get it open. I banged on the door but no one could hear me. There was a new *Readers Digest*, so I just relaxed and read a few articles. I tried the door again and it finally opened. So here I am.'"

Former Judge Gordon Melson talked about the time Melvin went to sleep during a theater production.

"We wondered what would happen if he didn't wake up

when it was over," he said, laughing.

Another member of Melvin's office staff is Thelma Arnold, who came to know him when her husband was one of Melvin's oil well pumpers. In 1996, Melvin's office manager, Suann Shepherd, became ill and Thelma offered to help out in her absence, and remained after Shepherd's death.

Shepherd occupied a special place in the Moran office. She had been office manager for Melvin's father in Tulsa, and came to Seminole when Meyer Moran died. When she died of cancer, Melvin had a special cornerstone installed in the museum next to the courtroom exhibit in her honor.

"I guess my perception of working as a secretary was to do my job and, for goodness sakes, don't bother the boss," Arnold said.

"My thoughts were that I should 'shield' him from unwanted phone calls, deflect unwanted visitors, and do my job without bothering him if at all possible.

"The only advice Suann gave me was if I had any problems at all to ask Melvin. I couldn't imagine at the time ever being comfortable enough in my job to ask him anything."

Arnold soon discovered that Melvin does not need or want to be shielded from anything or anyone. His only restriction is caused by lack of time.

Arnold's husband became ill in 1997 and died in 1998. "I have always been a basically angry person," she said. "Anger has always been my first reaction to almost any situation. If I was crying my eyes out, it was usually because I was so mad.

"You can imagine what kind of strain that kind of personality brings to a situation. And that was exacerbated by my husband's illness and subsequent death."

With other factors in play, Thelma found herself angry at everyone. Most people avoided her, but the people in the office were trapped. While many say they have never seen Melvin angry, never seen him use profanity, Arnold said she is one who has tested that theory completely.

"I don't remember a single incident, but I remember clearly that there were many incidents when I spat out angry words…ugly words," she said.

"And I remember seeing Melvin's face flush with anger. Sometimes he answered me, always kindly, and sometimes he just walked back into his office, but I'm just sure that his temper definitely flared.

"And each time this happened, I would wait for that other shoe to drop. I expected him to scold me, fire me, lecture me, shame me, avoid me…something. It never once happened."

What Arnold did see was Melvin leave her office, walk into his, then turn immediately and come back into her office.

"And every single time he walked back in, his anger never came back with him," she said, marveling at Melvin's self control.

Arnold said she has watched him for years and never seen him react negatively or angrily to anyone or any situation.

"That strength of character is indicative of Melvin Moran's core," she said. He has kindly pointed out mistakes she made — sometimes as dreadful as sending an important letter to the wrong person. But he has never lectured, scolded, shamed, or in any way tried to embarrass her.

"When he must show me a stupid mistake that I've made, he does it, but he doesn't make a big deal of it," she said.

Arnold said she believes Melvin's highest ambition is to make absolutely certain that no single employee has time to get bored or feel unnecessary. He once found that Arnold hated not being able to complete her "to dos" by quitting time, so he began giving her only what she could handle.

"Then as I got faster, he dictated more," she said. "He qualifies for the title 'efficiency expert.' However, we are all very comfortable in accepting personal calls at work and if we need a day off, all we have to do is ask."

Arnold is in a position to know that Melvin's wisdom is sought by people in very high places.

"He leads with the ease of a general," she said. "And yet he hustles over to the post office and stands in line to buy stamps when his three secretaries are so busy they don't have time. He truly is a person to whom no job is too large or too small."

Lana Reynolds, a vice president at Seminole State College, has worked closely with Melvin for years, first on college projects, for the Chamber of Commerce, and also as a member of the museum's board.

"His benevolence is legendary," she said. "The parties for the museum staff, the Rotary's Christmas dinner… he does all the shopping and he's there serving food from early in the morning until it's over.

"He hosts a steak dinner for our ball team, gives them gifts, plays games with them. It would be one thing to do this once, but these are annual events. And he's doing this for lots of others that we don't even know about."

Reynolds said she has heard high-ranking politicians, CEOs of major corporations, and state leaders of universities, foundations, and businesses all speak publicly of their respect for Melvin.

"Yet his humble manner and meek personality seem to cause him to be embarrassed by the praise so many people of importance lavish on him," she said.

"He has traveled the world and yet pours his heart and soul into his home community of Seminole. He is a great historian of how our town has grown and developed over the years, overcoming challenges and celebrating successes. He is a constant driving force for making things better for the future. His input in community affairs is always motivated by his love of Seminole and his desire to see good things happen here."

Former Seminole Chamber of Commerce Director Jenny Morgan said Melvin has been a force in the Chamber as well.

"When I came to the Chamber, he was the first person to come down and welcome me," she said. "He was so helpful. I'm not the most polished person in the world and he became my greatest mentor. I'd ask him how to handle this or that situation and he'd explain the dynamics of the situation and always give me such good advice. For a long time he'd come down every week to see if I needed anything and we'd talk over situations."

Morgan said she has heard people joke about his being the "peacemaker."

"I don't think it's a joke," she said. "He really does want to keep the peace. And he never wants anyone who contributed to be overlooked, whether they contributed dollars and cents or just constructive criticism."

"One of the best things about Melvin," Morgan said, "is the way he can correct someone so gently and tactfully that they actually thank him for it.

"His mind is constantly going from how this person feels to how that person feels so he can be sensitive to everyone's feelings," she said.

She talked about an experience when someone from out of town had made several unpleasant phone calls and an e-mail to the Chamber, blasting Seminole.

"I wrote back saying I didn't know why he felt so antagonistic about Seminole, but I'd be happy to discuss it with him if he would like to," Morgan said. "He wrote back even uglier than before.

"I forwarded it to Melvin and asked him what I could say to this guy. He wrote back and explained that, to some people, the word antagonistic might seem negative and that maybe that wasn't the right word to have used. And I realized he was right. His advice then was to just let it go, and it was the right advice."

She laughed about a funny story Melvin had told her.

"He's on the State Tourism Board and he was asked to come up and speak to these writers for the television program 'Saving Grace,'" Morgan said. The program is about an Oklahoma City policewoman, played by Holly Hunter.

"Melvin thought he ought to watch the program before he talked to the people. He saw it was for mature audiences. After he watched it, he told me he thought he must not be mature enough for it! But he talked to the writers and they came to Seminole and toured the museum. I think even Holly Hunter came and I understand they're going to do a program with the museum as a backdrop."

His business partner, Gene Rainbolt, said that, through all good times and the tough times, he and Melvin have always "been in the same harness: trying to improve things in Seminole, through the college, the museum...and then all of Oklahoma. Just like BancFirst's motto, 'Improving Oklahoma one community at a time.'"

Former Governor George Nigh said his memories of Melvin Moran are from their political campaigns together, the museum, and Melvin's love for Jasmine.

"Should you happen to go to *Webster's* [dictionary] and look up the word 'gentleman,' you surely would find the first words in the definition would be Melvin Moran," he said.

"That would be true no matter which way you looked it up, either as gentleman or gentle man.

"That statement is made upon years of personal observation and knowledge. That description has never wavered in any manner in all of his activities, be they personal, business, political, or public service.

"So many times in a biography, subject matter deals with fact, years, numbers or awards. That is historical and as it should be.

"But if you did not go beyond those areas, you would not know the real Melvin Moran. His concern has always been for his family, his friends, his neighbors, his hometown, his beloved state. That is the true strength of the man.

"While he indeed accomplished much, he did even more for others. What an inspiration!

"I am among the many who are honored to have benefited from his friendship and, yes, his caring. The future of Oklahoma has been made brighter by the past of Melvin Moran."

CHAPTER TWENTY-FOUR

A Place in the History Books

Melvin grew up in Seminole, through seventh grade, then graduated high school in Tulsa. After college in Missouri and a tour of duty in England with the United States Air Force, he returned to Seminole to begin working in his father's company.

"When I came back to Seminole in 1953, I remember going to the Owl Drug Store at the corner of Broadway and Second Street," Melvin said. "I ordered a Dr. Pepper. The drink was brought to me and the cost was five cents.

The Morans with singer Garth Brooks and Dave McCurdy in 1994.

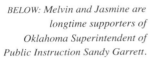

RIGHT: As a member of the Oklahoma Tourism Board, Melvin visited in 2007 with actress Holly Hunter and Nancy Miller, the creator and writer of the television series "Saving Grace."

BELOW: Melvin and Jasmine are longtime supporters of Oklahoma Superintendent of Public Instruction Sandy Garrett.

"On that particular day, I was not carrying that much cash on me, so I asked if I could write a check for the drink. The drugstore refused to take my check and I remember walking away thirsty, leaving the drink on the counter."

That could never happen to Melvin Moran in Seminole ever again. He has been named Seminole Citizen of the Year and to the Halls of Fame for Seminole, Tulsa Central High School, Oklahoma Higher Education, and for the state of Oklahoma, as well as the Oilman's Hall of Fame.

Today, after more than 50 years of public service, Melvin Moran is looked on throughout Seminole, the state, and much of the nation, as a father of the community. He is not only a leader, he is someone you would want to follow, someone warm and caring, someone you can go to for help, someone who has your best interests always at heart and, at the very end, who would move all the forces of earth, and even heaven, to help.

"How will the history books paint him? They'll miss most of it and that's fine with Melvin," said Robert Henry.

"What he has done has essentially been the anonymous donor giving to the anonymous donee – tzedakah. He has helped a lot of people through supporting idealist politicians, through the Children's Museum, all those charities, the Christmas dinners, scholarships, Oklahoma Arts Institutes.

"They don't know it was Melvin Moran who helped them, a lot of them, and never will."

Melvin met presidential candidate Barack Obama early in 2008 at the home of mutual friend, Tulsan George Kaiser. Obama became the first African American president of the United States in November, 2008.

Asked how Melvin's work at the museum might play in history, Henry said, "How do you evaluate the benefit to society of a child given the gift of imagination?

"That imagination may become a scientific theory or technological instrument. Or a play or a song or a novel.

"History will miss that. That's fine with Melvin, that's not why he does it. History will show him to be a brilliant, successful businessman with immaculate ethics. They'll say, 'Here is a man who realizes if you want more of something, you have to invest in it. If you want to get more imagination, creativity, education, culture, put money into those things.'

"This reflects his Jewish faith, which teaches that teaching children is as important as building a temple."

INDEX

Fortune Magazine 258
France 128
Frankfurt, Germany 179

G

Garrett, Sandy 291
Gazit, Schlomo 61, 126-130
Georgia 237
German language 172
German Revolutionary Cells (RZ) 127
Geselle, Michael 107-108, 226
Gettysburg Address 236
Gill, Don 222
Gill, Vince 192, 256
Gipson, Fred 195
Glenn, Anne 158
Glenn, John 158
Gore, Albert 233-235
Gore, Al 136
Governor's Advisory Council on
    Energy 258
Governor's Conference on Tourism
    203
Governor's Mansion 207
Grand Canyon 78
Great Pumpkin Event 203
Greater Seminole Oil Field 140,
    230-231
Green, Curtis 190
Gridiron Show 281
Grisso Mansion 123
Gusher Inn 198

H

Hamilton, Dan 266
Hamilton, Deanna 266
Hammer, Zevulum 61
Hammons, Robert 20, 22
Harber, Frank 146-147
Harborne, England 54
Harvest House restaurant 155
Havel, Vaclav 235-236
Hawaii 250

Hebrew 24, 31, 60, 172, 217
Heiman, Bob 131
Heiman, Joy 131
Henderson, Kenneth 123
Henry, Brad 6, 161, 206-207,
    227-229, 243
Henry, Jan 253
Henry, Kim 6, 205-208, 272
Henry, Robert 5, 87, 123, 130, 133,
    137-38, 154, 161, 199, 207-208,
    213, 223, 225, 232-235, 237,
    252-253, 256-259, 269, 277, 280,
    292-293
Herzberg, Arthur 74
Hillerman, Tony 256
Holdenville, Oklahoma 83
Holland 72
Holocaust 9, 17, 154
Honolulu, Hawaii 208, 249
Horace Mann Junior High 26, 30
Horn Church, England 63
Houston, Texas 31
Howell, Bob 83-84
Hunter, Holly 287-288, 291
Hutton, Barbara 55

I

Independent Petroleum Association
    of America 192, 258
Indiana State Chamber of Commerce
    165
Indiana Woman of the Year 165
Integris Baptist Medical Center
    206-207
Iron Curtain 243
Israel 7, 9, 11-12, 17, 46, 56, 59, 63,
    119, 122, 125, 127, 130-132, 174,
    217-219, 259
Israeli Air Force 128
Istook, Ernest, 239-243
Italia Conti school 65

J

Jacobson, Joseph 59-60, 124-126
James, Henry 268
Japan 234-235
Jasmine Moran Children's Museum 6, 171, 197-214, 219, 259, 263-264, 272, 282, 285, 292
Jayroe, Jane 176-179
Jefferson Memorial 236
Jerusalem, Israel 9, 13, 45, 59-60, 88, 90, 113, 118, 120, 123, 127-129, 217-219
"Jerusalem of Gold" 59, 217
Jewish 18, 24, 30, 31, 36, 56, 61, 154, 169, 171, 217, 276, 293
Johnson, Carlos 228
Johnson, Glen, 152
Johnston, Charles 195
Jones, Barbara 262, 280-281
Jones, Bob 262, 281-282
Jones, Les 99
Jones, Steve 242
Jordan 218
Judaism 11, 73
Judean Mountains, Israel 60
Juneau, Alaska 216

K

Kahn, Arthur 74
Kahn, Ella 24
Kahn, George 24, 32, 133
Kahn, Iris 21-22, 32
Kahn, Mike 133
Kaiser, George 292
Kansas City, Missouri 16, 31, 40
Kaska, Isaac 74
Kazakhstan 244, 247
Keating, Frank 44
Kelly, Tom 190
Kamay, Texas 23
Kennedy, John F. 179-180, 236
Kennedy, Ted 236
Kenya 128

Kerner, _____ 48
Kerr-McGee Corporation 200, 230-232
Kiesel, Allison 249-250
Kiesel, Ryan 249-250, 269-272
Keith Toby 270
King, Billie Jean 42
King, Martin Luther 112
Kleiman, Elisa Moran 8, 95-113, 139, 165-169, 255, 263
Kleiman, Gary 134, 165-169, 206
Knutsen, Lillian 57-58
Kleiman, Michelle 8, 169
Kleiman, Nicole 8, 169-170
Kohlberg, Kravis and Roberts Company 14
Koran, The 117
Korean War 12
Kremlin 245
KSLE radio station 195

L

Lafayette, Indiana 165
Lakenheath Base, England 48-50, 55
Landa, Norman 262-264
La Scala 67
Las Vegas, Nevada 78-79
Latvia 9, 11, 12, 14, 16, 21, 245
Lavendar, Ray 51
Lazy Days Parade 157
Lebow, Marvin 30
Levy, David 61
Lilly, Waldo 144-145, 150
Lincoln Memorial 236
London, England 46, 48, 52, 55, 57-58, 64-65, 67-68, 71, 73, 138-139
London Financial Times, The 258
Long, Gary 54
Long, Martha lease 82
Los Angeles, California 36
Lunch 'n' Such 204, 276

Moran, Meyer 9, 11-12, 14-18, 20,
   23-26, 29, 35-36, 40, 61, 71, 76,
   81, 122, 125, 156, 162, 283
Moran, Minnie 25
Moran K Oil 133, 258
Moran Oil Company 17, 133
Moran Oil Enterprises 133, 258
Moran Pipe and Supply 17, 23, 133,
   222, 226
Moran, Sidney 8, 11, 13, 17-20, 23-24,
   29-30, 35, 40, 47, 61, 121-122,
   134, 184, 278
Moran, Sonia 12, 17
Morgan, Jenny 286-288
Morgan, Suzy 138
Moscow, Soviet Union 244, 247
Mullen, Vernon 186
Muncie, Indiana 15
Muskogee, Oklahoma 25

N
Nairobi, Kenya 129
National Society of Fundraising
   Executives 257
Navon, Yitzhak 59, 61-62, 174-176
Nazis 12, 14, 233
Negev, Israel 62
New Jersey, Kilmer Base 49-50
Newly, Anthony 65
New Mexico, Albuquerque, Sandia
   Base 47, 49
Newmarket, England 51, 56
Newsweek Magazine 268
New York 35-36, 50-51, 72, 74-75,
   175, 244
New York Times 258
Nicklaus, Jack 187
Nigh, George 151, 158, 288-289
Norman, Oklahoma 190, 263
Nowata, Oklahoma 15
Northwood Elementary School 198
Nunn, Sam 237-239

O
Oakland Zoo 212
Obama, Barack 292
Oilman's Hall of Fame 291
Oklahoma 6, 58, 83, 79, 85, 98,
   102-103, 108, 127, 130-131,
   134-135, 137-140, 147, 184, 190,
   194, 202, 205, 210-211, 213-214,
   237, 250, 254, 259-260, 272, 282,
   288-289
Oklahoma Academy for State Goals
   13, 261
Oklahoma Arts Council 44
Oklahoma Arts Institute 257, 292
Oklahoma Bar Association 85
Oklahoma City, Oklahoma 22, 46,
   54, 78, 82, 85, 130, 158, 161,
   180-183, 210, 220, 231, 239,
   240-243, 254, 256, 287
Oklahoma County, Oklahoma 239
Oklahoma Hall of Fame 87, 192,
   252-260, 291
Oklahoma Heart Hospital 281
Oklahoma Higher Education Alumni
   Council 227-229; Hall of Fame
   291
Oklahoma House of Representatives
   228
Oklahoma Independent Petroleum
   Association 13, 137, 143, 190,
   192, 258
Oklahoma State Board of
   Equalization 138, 258
Oklahoma State Board of Regents
   151
Oklahoma State Capitol 142, 228
Oklahoma State Chamber of
   Commerce 260
Oklahoma Tourism Commission 179,
   287, 291
O'Leary, Hazel 137
Outstanding Attraction Award 203
Owl Drug Store 290

Watkins, Wes 158, 240-241
Weems, Sheila 250
West End, London, England 46, 65
West Germany 128
Wewoka, Oklahoma 195
White House 132, 135-136
Winfield House 55
Winnipeg, Canada 37
Winters, Jack 34
Women's Army Corps 55
Woolaroc 162
World War II 9, 12, 14, 17
Wright, Jim 164

Y
Yeager, Oklahoma 82
Yiddish language 172-174
YMCA 168-169
Yugoslavia 72